LISTOPIA

SPACE

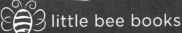

little bee books

An imprint of Bonnier Publishing Group
853 Broadway, New York, New York 10003

Author: Mike Goldsmith
Editor: Lydia Halliday
Designer: Allen Boe
Publisher: Donna Gregory

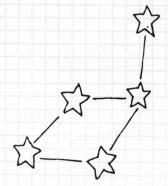

Manufactured in China 251215

First Edition 10 9 8 7 6 5 4 3 2 1

Library of Congress Cataloging-in-Publication data is
available upon request.

ISBN: 978-1-4998-0280-1

littlebeebooks.com
bonnierpublishing.com

CONTENTS

INTRODUCTION

When someone asks you what you did today, you'll list everything you did. When you talk about what you had for dinner last night, you'll list what you ate. When you don't turn your homework in, trust us . . . you'll have a list of excuses ready to go!

People naturally think of things in lists. You could say that the alphabet is a list of letters, or a dictionary is a list of words. Of course, you're on all sorts of lists, from your classroom list to your sports team roster. Lists are such a natural way of looking at the world that we decided to look at space using lists!

Our planet Earth, together with the Sun, Moon, planets, stars, and galaxies, exists in space. If you go out on a dark, moonless night away from city lights, you can see thousands of stars—but for each star you can see, there are billions that

you can't. Although many are brighter than the Sun, they're just too far away to see.

In this book, you can explore the mysteries and wonders of space, from the biggest planets to the brightest stars, the greatest spacecrafts to the strangest places on Mars, the most important milestones in space history to the most exciting future missions.

With space probes exploring the solar system, enormous new telescopes scanning the skies, astronauts working high overhead in the International Space Station, and new discoveries about the past and future of the Universe, there's never been a better time to explore space.

Read it through from front to back, or just open up a page at random. When you're done, check off all the items from this list that describe how you feel about this book.

MY LISTOPIA LIST

____ This book was amazing!

____ This was the best book ever!

____ I couldn't put this book down!

____ This book is a rectangle!

____ Please make more Listopia books!

Biggest Things in the Solar System

When the solar system formed more than 4 billion years ago, all there was to it was the Sun, dust, and gas. Some of the dust and gas stuck together as lumps, and some of the lumps stuck to others to form the planets, moons, and other larger objects. Yet there are still a lot more small objects going around the Sun than large ones.

10. Titan
(40% the size of Earth)
Mist-covered moon of Saturn.

9. Ganymede
(41% the size of Earth)
A moon of the planet Jupiter.

8. Mars
(53% the size of Earth)
The fourth planet from the Sun, and the most similar to Earth.

7. Venus
(95% the size of Earth)
Our closest planetary neighbor.

6. EARTH

Our homeland—3,958 miles in radius and the third planet from the Sun.

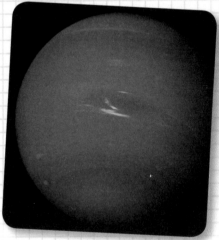

5. NEPTUNE
(3.9 TIMES BIGGER THAN EARTH)

The eighth and farthest planet from the Sun, discovered in 1846.

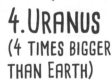

4. URANUS
(4 TIMES BIGGER THAN EARTH)

The seventh planet from the Sun, discovered by William Herschel in 1781.

3. SATURN

(9 TIMES BIGGER THAN EARTH)

Many people think Saturn is the most beautiful planet. It is the sixth planet from the Sun and the most distant planet you can see without a telescope or binoculars.

◀ RINGWORLD

Saturn's rings are made of trillions of icy bits of stone, each orbiting the planet. Although the rings are 186,411 miles across, they are less than 0.6 miles thick.

NOWHERE TO LAND

Saturn has no real surface. Under its deep, cold atmosphere is a mixture of liquids and gases, which get thicker with depth.

2. JUPITER
(11 TIMES BIGGER THAN EARTH)

It's impossible for a planet to get much bigger than Jupiter without becoming a star.

▲ **FLOATING WORLD**
Saturn weighs so little for its size that it would float in water.

POLAR MYSTERY
Around Saturn's north pole, the clouds form into a hexagon shape. No one is sure why this is.

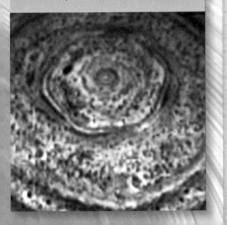

1. THE SUN
(109 TIMES BIGGER THAN EARTH)

The Sun is by far the largest object in the solar system. It is so huge that its mass makes up 99.8% of the solar system. A million Earth-sized objects could easily fit inside it.

11

SOLAR SYSTEM CONTENTS

The Earth goes around the Sun, and so do lots of other things, from giant planets to tiny grains of dust. Together, all these things make up the solar system ("solar" means "of the Sun"). It is the pull of the Sun's gravity that holds the solar system together. Here's what our solar system is made up of.

ONE STAR
THE SUN

It's about 4.6 billion years old, which means it's middle-aged.

EIGHT PLANETS

Out of these, our own planet, Earth, is third in order of distance from the Sun.

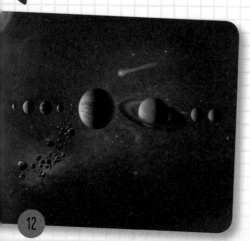

MANY MOONS

Most of the planets have moons—Earth has one, Mars has two, and the larger planets have dozens.

FOUR SETS OF RINGS

The four largest planets—Jupiter, Saturn, Uranus, and Neptune—each have a set of rings. Saturn's rings are by far the largest and brightest.

DWARF PLANETS

Like the other planets but unlike asteroids and smaller objects, dwarf planets are round (or fairly round) worlds that orbit around the Sun.

HAUMEA

A strange dwarf planet about twice as long as it is wide.

ERIS

Discovered in 2005, Eris is the largest dwarf planet—it is about 1,445 miles in diameter.

PLUTO

Considered to be a true planet until 2006, when astronomers decided it was a dwarf planet.

CERES

The closest dwarf planet to Earth. It is inside the asteroid belt.

ASTEROIDS

These are pieces of rock, some as big as countries, left over from the formation of the solar system.

COMETS

Huge lumps of rock, grit, and frozen gases that spend most of their time on the edge of the solar system. Occasionally they swoop in toward the Sun and become visible to us.

METEOROIDS

These are left-behind rocks and grit from long-dead comets. Meteoroids sometimes fall toward Earth, burning up as they pass through our atmosphere.

DUST
There is dust throughout the solar system so thinly spread that is it usually invisible.

GASES
The solar system contains lots of gas, but it is spread very thinly.

MOST FASCINATING SOLAR PHENOMENA

Our Sun, like all stars, is made of very hot gas. Its surface is constantly churning and changing, kept in motion by the energy boiling up from deep within. We see and feel this energy as sunlight.

10. CORONA

The corona is a sphere of very hot gas that surrounds the visible part of the Sun. The gas it is made from is so thin that it can only be seen when the rest of the Sun is hidden.

9. SOLAR WIND

The solar wind is a stream of fast-moving particles that spreads from the Sun through the whole solar system.

8. SPICULES

A spicule is a jet of gas that rises from the Sun. Because spicules are fairly cool, they are darker than their surroundings.

7. CORONAL MASS EJECTIONS (CMEs)

A CME is a huge bubble of superheated gas that is thrown off the Sun.

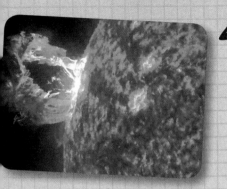

6. PROMINENCE

A prominence is a jet of glowing gas that rears up from the Sun, often reaching heights of thousands of miles.

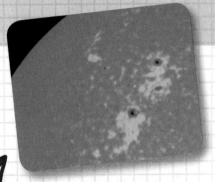

5. GRANULATION

When observed through special equipment, the surface of the Sun can be seen to be made of many tiny patches, called granules.

4. FACULAE

The granules are temporary raised areas on the Sun, with canyons between. Faculae are bright bursts of energy from deep within these canyons.

3. PLAGE

Plage means "beach," and these bright areas found at the edges of sunspots do look a bit like them.

2. FLARES

Flares are surges of brightness that affect small parts of the Sun's surface, appearing as bright spots.

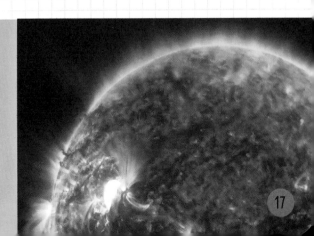

1.SUNSPOTS

Sunspots are by far the easiest solar phenomena to see from Earth, though special equipment must be used to do so—looking directly at the Sun can blind you.

BRIGHT DARKNESS ▶

The spots only look dark to us because they are a little less bright than their surroundings. If they could be seen without the rest of the Sun, they would glow brightly.

◀ MAGNETIC PAIRS

Sunspots are actually cooler regions on the solar surface. They have strong magnetic fields and usually appear in pairs.

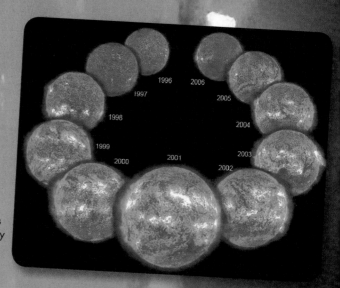

1996 2006
1997 2005
1998 2004
1999 2003
2000 2001 2002

SOLAR CYCLE ▶

Sometimes the Sun has no spots, and at other times it is very spotted. The Sun gets extremely spotty every eleven years.

WEATHER

The Earth's weather is affected by the activity on the Sun, and it goes through an eleven-year cycle too.

STRANGEST LUNAR MYTHS AND LEGENDS

Because the Moon is so easy to see, and also because it affects the tides of the Earth's seas, it has been the subject of myths and legends for thousands of years.

10. BLOOD MOON

When the Earth's shadow falls on the Moon (called a lunar eclipse), the Moon turns red. The Incas believed the red color was the Moon's blood, drawn when a giant jaguar attacked it.

9. LIFE ON THE MOON?

In 1835, the *New York Sun* newspaper made up a story that a powerful telescope had seen living creatures on the Moon. Many believed this "Great Moon Hoax," as it was called.

8. UNLUCKY CRESCENT

Some people used to believe it was unlucky to see the new crescent Moon through glass. No one is sure where this idea came from.

7. GOD OF EGYPT

Thoth was originally the ancient Egyptian god of the Moon, depicted as a man with the head of an animal. Later, he became god of knowledge.

6. LUNAR GODDESS

Chang'e is a Chinese goddess of the Moon. She is now the symbol of the Chinese Lunar Exploration Program.

5. SELENE

Selene is a moon goddess in the mythology of ancient Greece. The ancient Romans adopted her, giving her the name Luna.

3. LUNACY

In ancient Greece it was believed that the full moon made people act oddly. The word "lunacy" comes from the Greek word for moon.

2. WEREWOLVES

Many countries have legends about people who change into wild wolves when the Moon is bright. Today, there are lots of movies, books, and computer games that feature werewolves.

4. "ONCE IN A BLUE MOON"

This means a very rare event. Usually the Moon is full once a month. When there are two full moons in a month, the second one is called a "blue moon."

1. FACES IN THE MOON

The Moon is the only object in space with a surface that can be seen without a telescope, and there are many legends about the dark shapes that can be seen there.

OCEANS AND SEAS

Early astronomers thought that the dark areas were oceans, seas, and lakes. Now we know that they are great plains of cold, ancient lava.

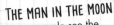

THE MAN IN THE MOON

Many people see the shapes in the Moon as a face. There are many stories and rhymes about this "Man in the Moon."

MOON SHAPES

There are many other shapes that can be seen—with a bit of imagination—in the Moon, including a crab, a man with his dog, an old woman with a bundle of sticks, a pair of hands, and a tree.

MOONS AND MINDS

Why do we see so many things in the Moon? It is because our brains have developed to recognize faces, people, and other objects even when they cannot be seen clearly, so sometimes we see things that aren't really there.

MOON RABBITS

The shapes on the moon look like a rabbit to some. In Japan and other East Asian countries there is a legend of a rabbit in the moon who pounds rice for making rice cakes.

23

Most Interesting
Lunar Features

The Moon is so much closer to us than any other space object, making it easier to study from Earth. Also, we have been there, and have explored some of it in person! So we have very good maps of the Moon, and we know a lot more about it than anything else in space.

10. The Lake of Death

A small dark area, made of old lava.

8. The South Pole-Aitken Basin

A huge depression—the deepest region on the Moon.

9. Tycho

The most spectacular lunar crater.

7. Straight Wall

An almost perfectly straight rille (groove), about 68 miles long.

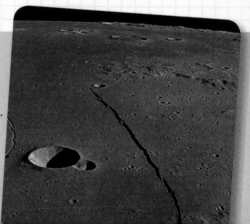

6. RUPES ALTAI

The largest cliff on the Moon, about 267 miles long.

5. MOUNT HUYGENS

The highest mountain on the Moon, about 3,280 feet tall.

4. SEA OF SHOWERS

The largest crater on the Moon, filled with cold, hard lava.

3. LUNAR APENNINES

A mountainous region, the last place on the Moon visited by humans.

2. SEA OF TRANQUILITY

The moon's seas are really large areas of cold lava, which look dark from Earth. The first humans on the Moon landed on the Sea of Tranquility in 1969.

1. ARISTARCHUS PLATEAU

A plateau is a high, flat area, and the oddly shaped Aristarchus plateau is the strangest place on the Moon.

ARISTARCHUS CRATER

The moon's craters were made by huge objects falling from space, millions of years ago. This crater, on the edge of the plateau, is one of the brightest on the Moon.

◄ COBRA HEAD

This is the bright white end of a valley called Vallis Schröteri, and it is thought to be made of material from the inside of the Moon, thrown out by a long-dead volcano.

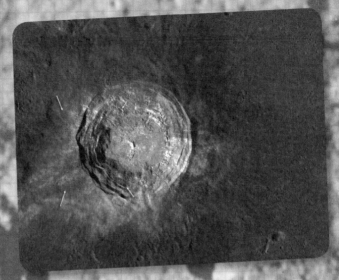

LUNAR LIGHTS ▶
Occasionally, red
and violet glows
have been seen on
the plateau. No
one knows what
they are.

◀ RADIOACTIVE CRATER?
When Apollo 15 passed
over Aristarchus in 1971,
radioactivity was detected,
and this may be related
to the other strange things
that have been seen there.

RECORD-BREAKING PLANETS

The solar system is a place of extremes—near the Sun, conditions are hot, and planets must orbit quickly to avoid being pulled down by the Sun's gravity. The farther outward you go, the colder things become.

LONGEST DAY:
VENUS

243 Earth days—longer than its year, which is 225 Earth days long.

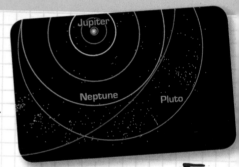

SHORTEST DAY:
JUPITER

9.8 Earth hours, so fast that Jupiter bulges out at the equator.

LONGEST YEAR:
NEPTUNE

165 Earth years. A human born there would die of old age before his or her first birthday.

SHORTEST YEAR:
MERCURY

88 Earth days. The year is short because Mercury moves quickly and is close to the Sun, so it doesn't have far to go around.

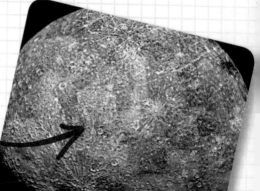

HIGHEST MOUNTAIN:
MARS

Olympus Mons,
approx.:
16 miles tall.

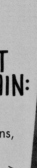

HOTTEST:
VENUS

864°F—hot enough to melt lead
and to boil sulfur.

COLDEST:
URANUS

−371.2°F. Although Neptune
is farther away from the Sun, it
makes some of its own heat.

LARGEST TEMPERATURE RANGE:
MERCURY

1,080°F—more than four
times the range on Earth.

BIGGEST CRATER:
MARS

Borealis Basin, 5,281 miles
in diameter.

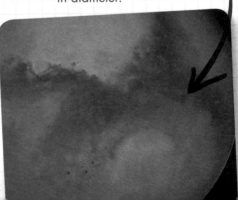

MOST MOONS: JUPITER

Nobody knows quite how many moons
Jupiter has, but 67 have been discovered
so far. Four are much brighter than the
rest and were discovered in the seventeenth
century by Galileo. They are still called the
Galilean moons.

GANYMEDE ▼
Made of rock and ice.

CALLISTO ▲
The most cratered moon
in the solar system.

Io ▼
The most volcanic place in the solar system.

EUROPA
Completely covered in ice and the smoothest moon of all.

STRANGEST MARTIAN PLACES

In our solar system, Mars is the planet most like Earth. It has been carefully studied for centuries, and more space probes have been sent there than anywhere else.

10. PHOBOS AND DEIMOS

These two tiny moons of Mars have names that mean "Fear" and "Terror."

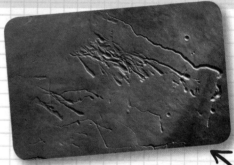

9. THE GREAT FACE

In 1976 an orbiting space probe took a photo of what looked like a face on Mars.

8. CARVED BY FIRE

What look like old river beds running down the side of the Pavonis Mons volcano are actually open-topped tunnels melted out by lava long ago.

7. DENTED PLANET

The Borealis Basin, probably the result of a collision with an asteroid, covers most of the northern part of Mars.

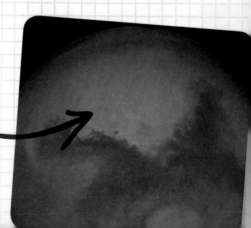

6. TRIPLE VOLCANO

Ascareus Mons, Pavonis Mons, and Arsta Mons are three volcanoes in a perfect row.

5. HIGHEST PEAK

Olympus Mons, an ancient volcano, is the highest peak on Mars at 84,000 feet.

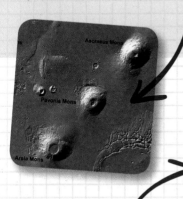

4. DRY ICE

Mars has ice caps that are made partly of "dry ice." This is formed of solid carbon dioxide gas.

3. THE HOURGLASS SEA

The first feature ever seen on Mars was a greenish patch, first thought to be a sea, then vegetation, and now dust. It is now called Syrtis Major.

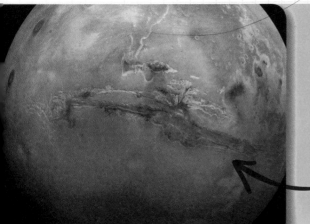

2. GRANDEST CANYON

Valles Marineris is the biggest canyon in the solar system at more than 2,500 miles long.

1. THE CANALS OF MARS

In the nineteenth century, astronomers saw a pattern of straight lines on Mars, which some thought must be artificial.

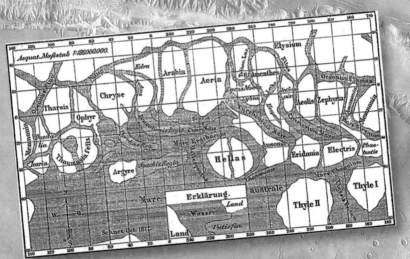

CANALI ▲
In 1877, the Italian astronomer Schiaparelli observed what he called "channels" on Mars. But the Italian word for channels is canali, so English-speaking astronomers thought that he had found waterways.

REAL CANALS
Although there are no canals on Mars, water did flow there once, and dry riverbeds remain.

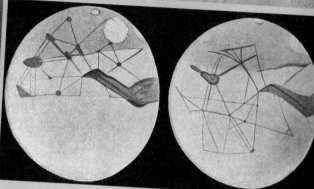

WORLD OF DROUGHT

In the USA, Percival Lowell made detailed maps of the canals. He thought they had been dug by Martians to make the most of their dwindling water supply.

THE MIND'S EYE

By the late twentieth century, space probes had found no trace of the canals. They had been an illusion, caused by badly used telescopes and good imaginations.

GREATEST SPACECRAFT

Spacecraft have always been at the cutting edge of technology, using the latest fuels, materials, and control systems to travel farther and faster into space.

10. FASTEST CRAFT

Juno, a spacecraft sent to explore Jupiter, will reach a velocity of 160,000 miles per hour (relative to Jupiter) in 2016.

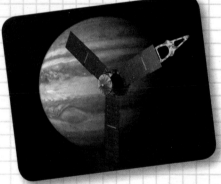

9. FASTEST LAUNCH

In 2006, *New Horizons*, a Pluto probe, was launched at the highest speed ever: 36,370 miles per hour.

8. PRIVATE VENTURE

SpaceShipOne became the first successful private space plane in 2004.

7. MAN IN ORBIT

Vostok 1 was the first manned spacecraft to orbit the Earth, in 1961.

6. FIRST INTO SPACE

The *V2 (A4)* was the first spacecraft, launched in 1942 as a weapon of war.

5. OLDEST IN SPACE

The *Proton* is the most successful launcher, first launched in 1965 and still in use today.

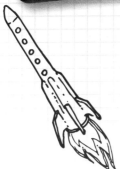

4. VINTAGE ROCKET

Russian *Soyuz* spacecraft, first launched in 1967, are still in use. They take astronauts to and from the International Space Station.

3. Reusable Craft

The Space Shuttle was a craft that took off like a rocket but landed as a plane does, and it could be used many times (unlike almost all other spacecraft). Six shuttles were built, and they were used for many jobs, from launching satellites to building the International Space Station. The first Space Shuttle launch was in 1981, and the last was in 2011.

1. Moon Flee

The Apollo missions, launched by the giant *Saturn V* rockets, took men to the Moon in the 1960s and 1970s.

2. Edge of Beyond

After exploring the outer planets, *Voyager 1* became the first spacecraft to leave the solar system in 2001.

◄ RECORD BREAKER

The *Saturn V* was the most powerful and biggest space rocket ever launched.

STEPS TO SPACE

*Saturn V*s are step rockets—they carry their fuel in several stages, which break off and fall back to Earth when they are empty.

Astronauts traveled in the Apollo modules—the Lunar Module, Service Module, and Command Module.

CLASSIC COMPUTER ►

The Apollo computer, very advanced for the time, was simpler than most watches are today.

LARGEST MOONS IN THE SOLAR SYSTEM

All the planets except for Mercury and Venus have at least one moon. Some of the moons in the solar system were asteroids, captured by gravity long ago.

10. OBERON
MOON OF URANUS

Named after the king of the fairies, 940 miles across (about 12% of Earth).

9. RHEA
MOON OF SATURN

Also called Saturn V (pronounced "five"), 950 miles across (about 12% of Earth).

8. TITANIA
MOON OF URANUS

With a surface that cracked when its core swelled up, 980 miles across (about 12% of Earth).

7. TRITON
MOON OF NEPTUNE

With ice volcanoes, 1,682 miles across (21% of Earth).

6. EUROPA
MOON OF JUPITER
With an underground ocean, 1,940 miles across (25% of Earth).

5. THE MOON
MOON OF EARTH
Earth's closest neighbor, 2,160 miles across (27% of Earth).

4. IO
HOT MOON OF JUPITER
2,260 miles across (29% of Earth).

3. CALLISTO
A MOON OF JUPITER
3,000 miles across (38% of Earth).

2. TITAN
CLOUDY MOON OF SATURN
3,200 miles across (40% of Earth).

VISITORS FROM EARTH
Titan was orbited by the *Cassini* probe in 2004, and *Huygens*, a lander carried by *Cassini*, reached its surface the next year.

◀ HIDDEN WORLD
Titan is covered in thick clouds, so its surface cannot be seen from Earth.

POISON SKY

Titan's atmosphere is made of chemicals like those in car exhausts.

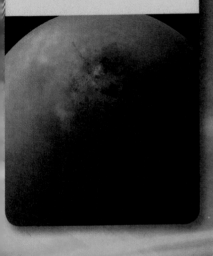

1. GANYMEDE
GIANT MOON OF JUPITER
3,270 miles across (41% of Earth).

▲ BLACK LAGOONS
The large seas on Titan are made of a thick, tar-like liquid.

COMETS

Beyond the planets are huge areas of space containing comets, which are mixtures of grit and ice. Sometimes, one of these will move toward the Sun. The Sun's heat melts some of the ice, which forms a tail. The comet will then go around the Sun over and over again, often taking centuries to go around each time.

CHURYUMOV— GERASIMENKO

Churyumov–Gerasimenko was the first comet to be landed on by a spacecraft (*Philae*, in 2014).

SCHWASSMANN— WACHMANN 3

Every time Schwassmann–Wachmann 3 returns, huge chunks break off this comet.

THE GREAT COMET OF 1864

The Great comet of 1864 will not return for 2,800,000 years. This is the longest period known for a comet.

SHOEMAKER— LEVY 9

Shoemaker–Levy 9 smashed into Jupiter in 1994.

KOHOUTEK

Kohoutek was the most disappointing comet ever. When it was discovered in 1973, it was expected to become extremely bright— but it remained very dim and hard to see.

ENCKE'S COMET

Encke's comet has one of the shortest known orbits around the sun—3.3 years—and the shortest of any comet visible to the naked eye. It will next be visible in 2017.

McNAUGHT

At its 2007 return, comet McNaught had a tail more than 139 million miles long, which is much farther than the distance between Earth and the Sun!

HALLEY'S COMET

Halley's comet is by far the most famous; it returns every 74 to 75 years, and each one of its visits since 240 BCE has been recorded.

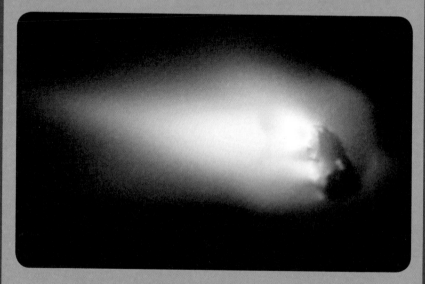

Halley last appeared in 1986, when it was visited by "The Halley Armada," a group of spacecraft from many countries.

Comets were thought to bring disaster to the Earth. The 1066 appearance of Halley's comet coincided with the death of England's King Harold. The death and the comet are both shown in the Bayeux Tapestry.

EDMOND HALLEY

In 1705 Edmond Halley figured out that many early reports were actually of the same comet. He correctly predicted when it would return, but died before it did.

In 1305 Giotto included a picture of Halley's comet in his painting "The Adoration of the Magi."

WILD 2

Particle samples from the "coma" (atmosphere) of this comet were collected by a spacecraft (Stardust), in 2004.

HALE–BOPP

Hale–Bopp became the brightest comet in living memory in 1997.

MOST FAMOUS
METEORITES

Meteoroids are pieces of grit and small lumps of metal or stone that travel through space. Sometimes they fall through our atmosphere, making bright streaks called meteors. Most burn up as they fall, but a few reach the Earth. They are then called meteorites.

THE SIKHOTE–ALIN

Iron meteorites arrived in 1947 in an explosion visible for over 200 miles.

TUNGUSKA EVENT

A huge meteoroid exploded over Siberia in 1908, flattening 830 square miles of trees.

TOMANOWOS

This iron meteorite is sacred to the Clackamas, a Native American tribe.

MURCHISON

This meteorite contains many chemicals called amino acids, the building blocks of life.

ANN HODGES

A meteorite hit Ann Hodges in Alabama in 1954. She is the only person known for sure to have ever been hit by a meteorite.

HOBA

This meteorite weighs about 145,000 pounds, making it the heaviest ever found. It was found in 1920 in Namibia, but it probably arrived on Earth about 80,000 years before that.

ALLENDE

This meteorite weighed many thousands of pounds on impact. Many of its shattered fragments are coated in natural glass and contain tiny diamonds.

THE BLACK STONE OF MECCA

Sacred to Muslims, this is probably a meteorite.

THE ALAN HILLS A81005

This meteorite originated on the Moon. It may have been blasted toward the Earth when a huge meteoroid crashed down.

ALH84001

ALH84001 is a meteorite from Mars, believed by some to contain fossilized Martian bacteria.

ALH84001▼
It was probably thrown up from Mars into space as the result of a meteoroid strike 17 million years ago. It reached Earth about 13,000 years ago.

In 1996 it was reported that the meteorite contained the fossils of tiny living things. The story made headline news, and President Clinton of the USA announced the importance of the discovery.

It is still not certain whether the shapes in the meteorite are fossils or not. Many say they are too small to ever have been alive.

FOUND IN ANTARCTICA
Like many meteorites, ALH84001 was found in Antarctica, where it could be seen easily against the ice and snow.

EARLIEST SPACESHIP IDEAS

The first spaceships blasted off into space in the 1940s—but people had been thinking up ways to fly through space for thousands of years before that. Nearly all of them were thought up by writers, and nearly all of them were headed for the Moon.

In Jules Verne's novels *From the Earth to the Moon* (1865) and *All Around the Moon* (1870), a capsule with astronauts on board is fired toward the Moon by an enormous cannon.

10. 1901
GRAVITY SHIELD

One of the cleverest ideas for traveling through space was to cut off the pull of Earth's gravity from the spacecraft. This was suggested by H. G. Wells in *The First Men in the Moon*.

9. 1865
SPACE ROCKETS

Achille Eyraud's *Voyage to Venus* was the first suggestion of a real space rocket, although many of the details were not correct.

8. 1865 CANNON

DEADLY JOURNEY
Actually, a trip like the one Verne suggested would kill the astronauts immediately, flattening them inside the capsule.

◄REACTION ROCKETS

One of Verne's best predictions was that rockets would be used to steer spacecraft.

INSPIRATIONAL WRITING

Verne's books were read by many scientists and engineers and helped to inspire actual missions.

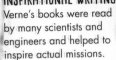

A CENTURY LATER . . .

In 1969, three men really did travel from Florida in a cylindrical capsule to the Moon and splashed down in the ocean on their return, just as Verne predicted.

7. 1835
BALLOON

Edgar Allan Poe's story *The Unparalleled Adventure of One Hans Pfaall* is about a journey to the Moon by balloon.

· 6. 1705
ROCKET-POWERED WINGS

In his book *The Consolidator*, Daniel Defoe's hero flies to the Moon using rocket-powered flapping wings. This was the first time rockets were suggested for a space vehicle.

5. 1703
CATAPULT

A giant catapult with powerful springs attached was suggested by English writer David Russen.

4. 1649
EVAPORATING DEW

Cyrano de Bergerac, in his book *Voyage to the Moon*, suggested that if dew was collected in glasses and the glasses attached to a jacket, the Sun would draw the dew up into space, taking the person wearing the jacket with it.

3. 1649
FIRECRACKERS

Cyrano de Bergerac's book had another way to get into space; a box pushed along by firecrackers (the first example of a solid-fueled spacecraft).

2. 1010
EAGLE-POWERED THRONE

Firdausi, the Persian writer of *A Book of Kings*, suggested that if a piece of meat were dangled in front of a powerful eagle, and the eagle harnessed to a throne, the bird could pull the throne to the Moon.

1. 2ND CENTURY CE
GIANT WATERSPOUT

The earliest tale of a trip to space was written more than 2,000 years ago by Lucian of Samosata, an ancient Greek writer. In it, a ship travels to the Moon by means of a waterspout—a powerful, twisting sea storm.

Best SPACECRAFT ENGINES

All spacecraft use rockets (with either solid or liquid fuel) to leave Earth, but once they are in space they can use many other ways to travel to their destinations. Some of these methods have not yet been tried.

SOLID FUEL

This is powerful and simple to use, but hard to control. So that it can burn without air, special chemicals called oxidizers are mixed into it.

LIQUID FUEL

Liquid fuel is carried in tanks and mixed with oxygen when it is ready to use. Kerosene is a popular liquid fuel.

SPACE PROBES

As they often swoop close to planets, space probes can use the gravitational pull to speed themselves on their way (this is called a slingshot effect).

NUCLEAR ENERGY

This has been suggested as a powerful spacecraft fuel but is considered too dangerous to use.

LASER POWER

In the future, powerful lasers in orbit around Earth may be used to push spacecraft through space.

THE SABRE

This is a powerful new drive that uses a jet to work in the atmosphere and a rocket to fly through space.

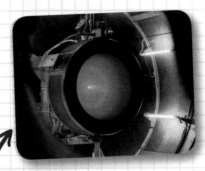

SOLAR SAILS

These are pushed along by the power of sunlight.

ION DRIVE

In an ion drive, atoms are split into parts called electrons and ions. Magnets are used to push a stream of ions into space, thrusting the craft in the opposite direction.

ANTIMATTER

As well as the matter that you and everything you can see are made up of, there is also antimatter, which can be made in laboratories. If matter and antimatter meet, they release enormous energy. This would make the most powerful engines of all.

INTERSTELLAR RAMJET

One day, people may travel to other stars, and they might use an interstellar ramjet to get there.

SOLVING THE FUEL PROBLEM

The heaviest thing a spacecraft carries is usually its fuel. The ramjet sucks in gas from the space around it and uses that instead.

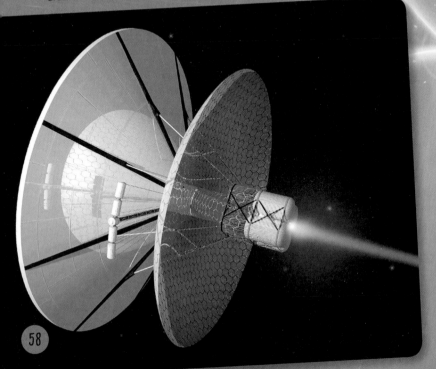

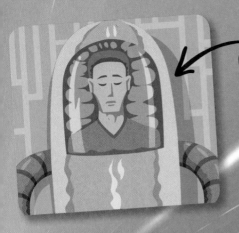

COLD SLEEP
Scientists think it may be possible to deep-chill astronauts so that they can "sleep" for years, hardly breathing. This would save food and air and stop them from getting bored.

LONG TRIPS
The ramjet would still take many years to reach other stars. It takes light over 4 years to travel from the nearest star and the ramjet would travel much slower than light.

SHUTTLING TO LAND
The ramjet would be too big to land on planets. Instead, astronauts would land on planets in shuttle craft.

Most Successful
Space Probes

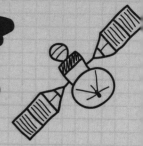

While astronauts have traveled no farther than the Moon, space probes have visited every planet in the solar system and many other objects too, including moons, comets, and asteroids.

10. New Horizons

New Horizons was the first mission to explore Pluto (in 2015) and the outer solar system.

9. Cassini/Huygens

The *Cassini* probe was the first to orbit Saturn's moon Titan (2004), and the lander it took with it, *Huygens*, was the first to land there (2005).

8. Messenger

Flew past Mercury in 2008, went into orbit around it in 2012, and finally crashed into the planet in 2015.

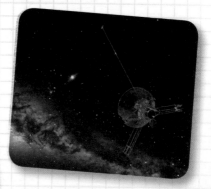

7. Pioneers

Pioneers 10 and 11 were the first probes to visit and photograph Jupiter and Saturn.

6. DAWN

The *Dawn* spacecraft was the first to reach a dwarf planet (Ceres, in 2015), and it also explored an asteroid (Vesta, in 2011).

5. VIKINGS

The twin *Viking* landers arrived on Mars in 1976 and took the first photos from the surface. They had robot arms to help them test the soil for life.

4. GIOTTO

The *Giotto* probe took photos of the core of Halley's comet in 1986.

3. LUNA 3

Until *Luna 3* traveled behind the Moon and sent photos back to Earth in 1959, no one knew what it looked like on the far side of the Moon.

2. VENERA 13 AND 14

The atmosphere of Venus is so hot and thick that all the spacecraft sent to land there have been destroyed. But in 1981 *Venera* 13 and 14 managed to send back data and images first.

1.VOYAGERS

The twin *Voyager* spacecraft explored the giant planets from the 1970s to the 1990s.

▼ GRAND TOURS

In the 1960s it was realized that many of the planets would soon line up, so that a single spacecraft could visit them all. Such voyages were called "Grand Tours."

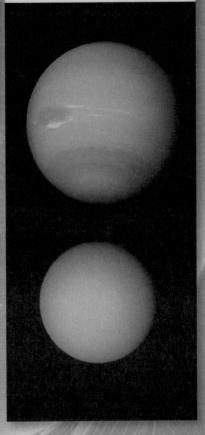

NEWS FROM SPACE
The probes discovered many new moons and features and sent back the first clear images of Uranus and Neptune.

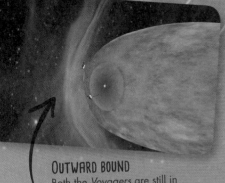

▲ SPACE TWINS
Voyager 1 explored Jupiter and Saturn, and the identical *Voyager 2* explored Uranus and Neptune.

OUTWARD BOUND
Both the *Voyagers* are still in space, on their way to distant stars, but they will not arrive for thousands of years.

GREATEST ROBOT EXPLORERS

To explore other worlds, robots have many advantages over people—they can cope with long periods in space, they need no air to breathe, they are tougher, and they do not need to return to Earth.

10. CURIOSITY

By far the largest Martian rover, *Curiosity* is a six-wheeled robot the size of a large car.

9. SPIRIT

The *Spirit* Mars rover was the first to find good evidence of water on Mars in 2004.

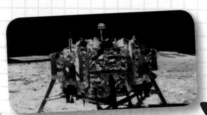

8. CHANG'E 3

Chang'e 3 is a Chinese lunar rover that arrived on the Moon in 2012.

7. UNDERWATER EXPLORER

Still at the planning stage, an underwater robot is being developed to explore the underground seas on Jupiter's moon Europa.

6. LUNOKHOD 2

The second lunar rover, *Lunokhod 2*, sent over 80,000 pictures of the Moon back to Earth.

5. LUNOKHOD 1

The first robot rover, which explored the Moon from November 1970 to September 1971, and traveled 6 miles.

4. SOJOURNER

Sojourner was the first robot rover on Mars, exploring the planet from July to September 1997.

3. iSTRUCT

iStruct is an ape-like robot being developed for future exploration of the Moon.

2. VIKINGS

Twin landers that searched for life on Mars in 1976. Though unable to move around, they sampled the soil using robotic arms and on-board laboratories.

1. OPPORTUNITY

Opportunity is a record-breaking Martian rover which worked for over 10 years and traveled more than 24 miles over the surface.

▼ **SMART ROBOT**
Opportunity was artificially intelligent and able to make simple decisions for itself.

PAST RETIREMENT

Opportunity's mission was planned to last 90 Martian days. It actually continued for over 4,100.

▼ DISCOVERIES

As well as finding evidence of water on Mars, *Opportunity* also discovered a meteorite—the first ever found on another planet.

▼ MISSION TO MARS

Opportunity was launched from Earth on July 7, 2003, and arrived on January 25, 2005.

SPACE JOBS

Not many people become astronauts, but many thousands have space-related jobs. Almost all need excellent science qualifications, but everyone who has any of the jobs in this list thinks they have the best job in the world!

10. SPACE PSYCHOLOGIST

Space travel has many effects on people's mind, so space psychologists are employed to help look after the crews on space missions.

9. ROCKET ENGINEER

A spacecraft is an enormous engineering challenge, and each one needs dozens of rocket engineers to build it.

8. ROBOTICIST

Robots have many jobs to do in space, from the rovers that explore other planets to arms that hold satellites for repair. They are built and looked after by roboticists.

7. PLANETARY SCIENTIST

Geology is the study of the Earth's structure, and planetary scientists study the geology of other worlds.

6. MISSION CONTROLLER

Space missions are complicated projects, and each is looked after by its own mission controller.

5. EXOBIOLOGIST

An exobiologist tries to figure out what alien life forms might be like.

4. Cosmologist

"Cosmos" is another name for "universe"—which means everything that exists. So that's what cosmologists study.

Cosmologists study the way the whole universe works, how it started, and how it will end.

Big Bang

All cosmologists agree that the universe started about 13.7 billion years ago as a sudden expansion called the Big Bang.

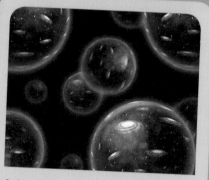

Many Universes

Cosmologists have many different theories about the universe. One is that our universe is just part of a much larger Multiverse, which we cannot see.

Master Mathematicians

Cosmologists are expert mathematicians and usually use powerful computers to help them.

3. ASTROPHYSICISTS

Astrophysicists apply the laws of physics to stars and other space objects to find out how they work.

2. ASTRONOMERS

Astronomers study the planets and stars, either by observing them or by using mathematics to figure out things about them.

1. ASTRONAUTS

Astronauts are the people who travel into orbit around the Earth or beyond.

GROUNDBREAKING ASTRONAUTS

The job of an astronaut is one of the most exciting on Earth—and off of it. Astronauts need many different skills and just the right sort of personality to do their jobs. They must also be very fit and healthy, and before blasting off they must undergo intense training.

10. DENNIS TITO
(USA)

The first space tourist (on the International Space Station, 2001).

9. VALERI POLYAKOV
(RUSSIAN)

Made the longest space flight: 437 days (1994–1995).

8. SVETLANA SAVITSKAYA
(RUSSIAN)

The second woman in space (1982).

7. Eugene Cernan
(USA)

The last human on
the Moon (1972).

6. Buzz Aldrin
(USA)

The second human
on the Moon (1969).

5. Neil Armstrong
(USA)

The first human on
the Moon (1969).

▲ SELECTION
Neil Armstrong was a member of
the US Navy and an expert pilot.
He went through hundreds of
tests and interviews before being
selected as an astronaut.

FIRST WORDS

When Armstrong stepped down from the Apollo module to the Moon's surface, his first words were "That's one small step for a man, one giant leap for mankind."

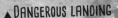
▲ DANGEROUS LANDING

Along with fellow astronaut Buzz Aldrin, Armstrong landed on the Moon in 1969. But Armstrong only found a suitable landing spot just before the fuel ran out.

FAME

As soon as it was known that Armstrong was to be first man on the Moon, he became world famous. About 600 million people watched on live TV as he stepped onto the Moon.

4. ALEXEY LEONOV
(RUSSIAN)

The first person to walk in space (1965).

3. VALENTINA TERESHKOVA
(RUSSIAN)

The first woman in space (1963).

2. JOHN GLENN
(USA)

The first American in space (1962), and, in 1998 when he was 77, he then became the oldest person in space.

1. YURI GAGARIN
(RUSSIAN)

The first human in space. On April 12, 1961, he orbited the Earth in his space capsule.

MOST VITAL
SPACESUIT PARTS

Most spacesuits cost millions of dollars and are almost like mini-space capsules, keeping their wearers alive and helping them to work in space.

10. SHIELDING

Space is full of dangerous radiation, so spacesuits contain special layers to protect the wearer.

9. COMMUNICATORS

Microphones and loudspeakers are connected either to radio systems or wires to keep astronauts in touch with each other.

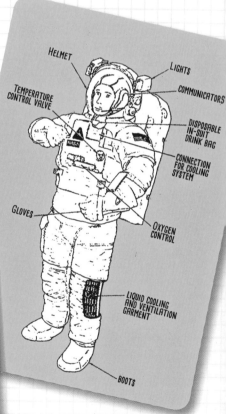

HELMET

LIGHTS

TEMPERATURE CONTROL VALVE

COMMUNICATORS

DISPOSABLE IN-SUIT DRINK BAG

CONNECTION FOR COOLING SYSTEM

GLOVES

OXYGEN CONTROL

LIQUID COOLING AND VENTILATION GARMENT

BOOTS

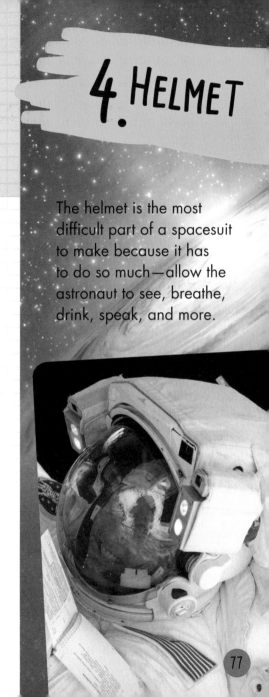

8. URINE COLLECTORS

It takes many hours to get into or out of a suit, so urine must be collected from inside.

7. WATER SUPPLY

Astronauts may have to spend many hours in their spacesuits, so drinking water is essential.

6. MONITORING

To make sure the astronaut is well, his or her breathing, heartbeat, blood pressure, and temperature are all checked by the spacesuit.

5. GLOVES

Gloves on spacesuits are a challenge, because unless they are flexible and fairly thin, they would be impossible to use. But they must protect the astronauts too.

4. HELMET

The helmet is the most difficult part of a spacesuit to make because it has to do so much—allow the astronaut to see, breathe, drink, speak, and more.

APOLLO HELMETS
Apollo astronauts had helmets that were specially designed for exploring the Moon.

Yuri Gagarin's helmet was simple and basic because he did not have to leave his capsule.

Alexey Leonov's helmet was the first to be used in space.

The helmet of an ISS astronaut is made of the most advanced materials.

3. Cooling system

Normally, the air around us carries away the heat our bodies produce, but in space the spacesuit needs to cool the astronaut down.

2. Pressurization layers

There is no air pressure in space, so anyone not wearing a pressurized suit would bloat and their blood would start to boil.

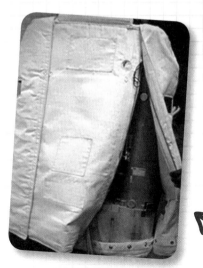

1. Oxygen system

Without oxygen to breathe, an astronaut would die in seconds.

FIRST ANIMALS IN SPACE

Animals were sent into space before the first astronauts to see whether living creatures could survive there. Most early animal space travelers died on their journeys, but as spacecraft design improved, more and more survived.

10. 1961 (USSR)

Guinea pig on Korabl-Sputnik 4. Returned safely to Earth.

Ham was the first animal to carry out any tasks in space, pressing buttons for rewards.

Ham wore a spacesuit, which saved his life when his capsule lost pressure.

After his return, Ham lived for the rest of his life in a zoo.

9. 1961 (USA)

Chimpanzee (Ham) aboard a Mercury capsule. Returned safely to Earth.

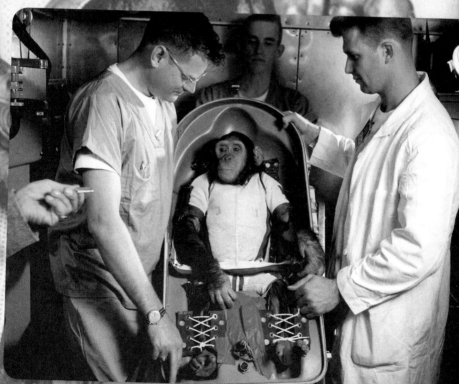

▲ **SELECTION**
Ham was chosen from a group of 40 chimpanzees, as he was fit, healthy, intelligent, and friendly.

8. 1960
(USSR)

Rats aboard *Sputnik 5*.
Returned safely to Earth.

7. 1959
(USA)

Frogs in Jupiter rocket.
Died during the launch.

6. 1959
(USSR)

Rabbit (Marfusa)
in R2 rocket.
Recovered alive.

5. 1958
(USA)

Squirrel monkey in the
cone of a Jupiter rocket.
Died after splashdown in
the south Atlantic.

4. 1957
(USSR)

Dog (Laika) aboard
Sputnik 2. Died
soon after launch.

3. 1950
(USA)

Mouse aboard V2
rocket. Died on the
way down to Earth.

2. 1949
(USA)

Rhesus monkey (Albert) aboard
V2 rocket. Albert died on his
way back to Earth.

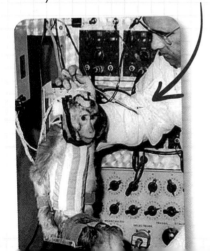

1. 1947
(USA)

Fruit flies aboard V2 rocket.
Returned safely home.

Achievements of Space-Going Nations

Space exploration began as a competition between the USA and the former USSR. Though many countries prefer to explore space alone, big missions are so expensive that nations must join together to fund them.

10. Czechoslovakia

Vladimír Remek, a Czech, was the first space traveler from a country other than the USSR or USA.

9. UK

The UK's greatest space triumph was to launch its own satellite (*Prospero*) using its own rocket (*Black Arrow*) in 1971.

8. Australia

In the 1960s, many countries launched spacecraft from Australia, which launched its own satellites too, because it is sparsely populated. Recently the country has decided to return to space exploration.

7. France

European nations now work together to explore space through the European Space Agency (ESA). France is encouraging ESA to do more, including exploring the Moon and Mars.

6. INDIA

As well as launching many satellites, India has sent unmanned missions to the Moon and Mars.

5. JAPAN

Many satellites are Japanese, and Japan is planning a crewed mission to the Moon. It has already sent a robot probe there.

4. GERMANY

The first technology for space exploration, as well as some of the best rocket scientists, came from Germany following the Second World War.

3. CHINA

Spaceman Yang Liwei was successfully launched into space on Chinese spacecraft *Shenzhou 5* in 2005. This made China the third space-traveling nation.

2. USSR

The former USSR launched the first successful satellite (Sputnik) and the first astronaut (Yuri Gagarin) into space. They also had the first space station and reached the Moon first.

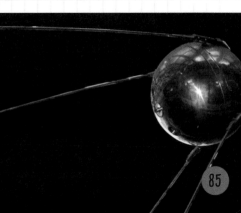

1. USA

The USA is by far the most successful space-going nation today.

SPACE PRESIDENT

President John F. Kennedy believed it was very important for the USA to explore space, and in 1961 he announced that Americans would soon go to the Moon.

▲ NASA
The National Aeronautics and Space Administration is the organization in charge of American space missions.

USA TODAY
The USA still sends many space probes, satellites, and people into space.

The Space Race
In the 1960s, the USA competed with the USSR to send people to the Moon. The USA won the space race in 1969.

GREATEST DANGERS
IN SPACE

Human beings are used to living on Earth, and we rely on it to provide us with air and food and to protect us from rays and objects from space. In space, technology must do these jobs instead, but many dangers still remain.

10. SABOTAGE

Because space missions attract a lot of publicity, there are suspicions that enemies of the countries that make them want to sabotage their spacecraft.

9. DRIFTING

Astronauts working outside their craft are tethered to them. If the tether should break and the astronaut drift away, they would be unable to make their way back.

8. SPACESUIT DAMAGE

When astronauts venture outside their craft, their spacesuits keep them alive. A puncture could prove fatal.

7. METEOROID IMPACT

Millions of meteoroids hurtle toward Earth every day. The atmosphere protects us from them, but if one hit a space vehicle, the vehicle would be easily destroyed.

6. Space junk collision

Many thousands of bits of old space technology orbit the Earth. Even small pieces move fast enough to destroy a spacecraft.

5. Computer viruses

Today's missions rely completely on computers for navigation and control. A computer virus could literally be deadly.

4. System failure

If a spacecraft's air supply, heating, cooling, or pressurization system should fail, it would soon become uninhabitable.

3. Re-entry

If a returning spacecraft simply fell through the atmosphere, it would burn up. Re-entry must be carried out slowly and with great care to keep the crew alive.

2. Launch

The most dangerous part of a space mission is the launch, when tons of fuel burn away in seconds.

1. RADIATION

The more radiation people are exposed to, the more likely they are to get cancer. The Sun produces a great deal of this radiation, and some comes from distant stars too. On Earth, the atmosphere shields us from most of this, although it is still dangerous to spend too much time in the Sun without protection. In space, the danger is far greater, especially when there is a storm on the Sun.

RADIATION DANGERS

Radiation burns the skin in the short term, weakens the blood in the medium term, and causes cancers in the long term.

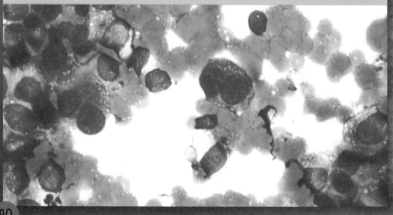

▲ DEADLY SUNLIGHT
The Earth's atmosphere shields us from radiation from the Sun (especially ultraviolet) which would kill an unprotected space traveler.

◄ COSMIC RAYS
Deadly X-rays and gamma rays bombard space travelers from deep space.

◄ PROTECTION
The best way to protect astronauts is to use metal shields, but really good ones are too heavy to take into space.

GROUNDBREAKING SATELLITES AND SPACE STATIONS

Modern life relies on satellites for phone calls, TV, weather forecasting, navigation, and much more. Since 1971, one of these satellites has usually had people on board: a space station.

10. ISS

ISS, the biggest space station (1998).

8. GPS

GPS satellites are what makes navigation systems work (1973).

9. SKYLAB

Skylab, the first US space station (1973).

7. SALYUT 1

Salyut 1, the first space station (1971).

5. TRANSIT 1B
Transit 1B, the first successful navigation satellite (1960).

6. TELSTAR
Telstar, the first TV and phone satellite (1962).

4. TIROS 1
Tiros 1, the first successful weather satellite (1960).

2. EXPLORER 1
Explorer 1, the first US satellite (1958).

3. VANGUARD 1
Vanguard 1, the oldest satellite still in orbit (1958).

1. SPUTNIK 1

Sputnik 1 was the first satellite, launched from Russia on October 4, 1957. It orbited Earth until January 1958, when it fell back to Earth again. For several weeks, it transmitted radio signals which could be picked up all over the planet.

SIMPLE DESIGN

Sputnik was designed to be as simple as possible. It was a metal sphere that carried only a radio transmitter, aerials, power supply, and heat control.

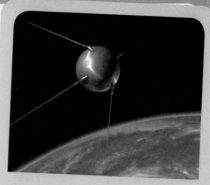

AROUND THE EARTH

Over three months, *Sputnik* made 1,350 Earth orbits. Its orbit was oval-shaped, so its altitude varied from 133.6 miles to 583.5 miles.

WORLD FAMOUS

Sputnik's signals could be picked up by radios all over the world. The Americans were shocked to have been beaten to orbit by the Soviets.

FIERY END

Sputnik was not high enough to escape completely from the Earth's atmosphere, which gradually slowed it down until it fell back toward Earth, burning up on the way down.

Most Important Parts of the
International Space Station

The International Space Station (ISS) is the largest spacecraft ever built. It's so big that it had to be constructed from many separate parts (most are called modules), with each sent up on its own rocket. It has been continuously crewed since 2000.

10. Radiators

The Sun makes the ISS very hot, so it uses large radiator panels to get rid of the excess heat.

9. Integrated Truss Structure

The connecting structure onto which all the modules and other parts of the ISS are fixed.

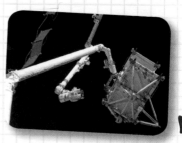

8. Solar Panels

Solar panels, arranged in four arrays, provide the ISS with as much electricity as is used by about 40 houses on Earth.

7. Canadarm 2

A giant robotic arm, used for moving parts of the ISS or other large objects around.

6. KIBO

The largest module, used for many different types of scientific research.

5. CUPOLA

Observatory with seven windows to observe the Earth.

4. AIRLOCKS

There are three airlocks on the ISS, called Poisk, Pers, and Quest, enabling astronauts to safely pass from the spacecraft out into space.

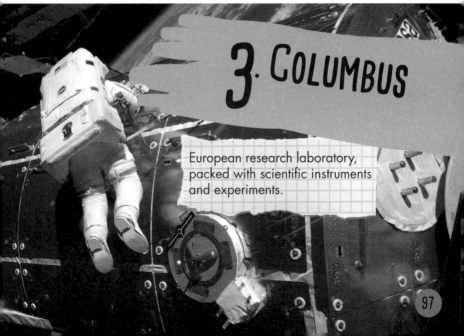

3. COLUMBUS

European research laboratory, packed with scientific instruments and experiments.

Materials International Space Station Experiment (MISSE)

Studies the effects of space on materials.

▼ Atomic Clock Ensemble in Space
A super-accurate clock system, designed to investigate the nature of time.

▲ **SOLAR MONITORING OBSERVATORY**
To measure and study the Sun.

European Technology Exposure Facility, clamped to the outside of Columbus to carry out experiments in unprotected space.

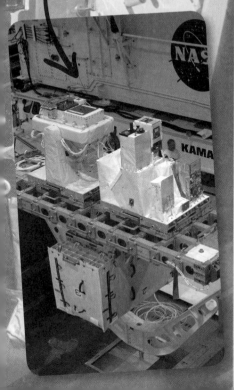

2. ZVEZDA

First inhabitable module. Equipped with engines to keep the ISS in place.

1. ZARYA

The first module to arrive, in 1998. Now used for storage.

99

MOST SIGNIFICANT MILESTONES IN SPACE HISTORY

Exploring space needs breakthroughs by many kinds of experts, including scientists, inventors, and engineers. Slow at first, the development of space technology became very rapid from the 1960s onward.

10. MAN-MADE OBJECT LEAVES THE SOLAR SYSTEM

The *Voyager 1* probe, launched in 1977, left the solar system in 2012. It is now more than 6 billion miles from Earth.

9. PERMANENT SETTLEMENT IN SPACE

Since 2000, there have always been some astronauts on the ISS. The plan is that space will never again be empty of humans.

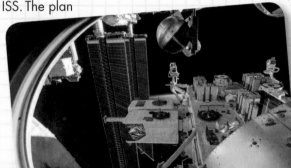

6. INTERPLANETARY MISSION

Mariner 2 was the first space probe to explore another planet, Venus. It was launched in 1962.

8. PEOPLE ON THE MOON

The American Apollo 11 mission took the first humans to the Moon's surface in 1969.

7. SOFT LANDING

The Soviet probe, Luna 6, became the first spacecraft to land on the Moon without breaking up, in 1966.

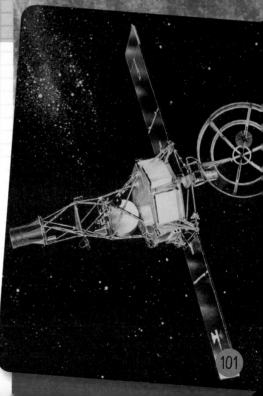

Backup ship

Mariner 2 was a replacement for *Mariner 1*, which had to be blown up after a computer error sent it off course.

▼ Discoveries

The probe measured the mass and temperature of Venus.

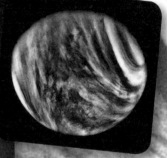

Long journey

The probe took 109 days to reach Venus. It studied space dust and solar activity on its journey.

▶ Design

Mariner 2 had a hexagonal core, a mast, and a boom containing scientific instruments and twin solar panels. President Kennedy received a model of *Mariner 2* from NASA.

5. PEOPLE IN SPACE

Yuri Gagarin became the first cosmonaut (Russian version of "astronaut") in 1961.

4. FIRST SPACECRAFT

V2s were war rockets designed to destroy enemy cities. In 1942, one traveled into space on its way to attack London.

3. LAW OF GRAVITY

Isaac Newton published his Law of Universal Gravitation in 1687.

2. EARTH IS A PLANET

Copernicus published a book in 1543 arguing that the Earth was a planet and orbited the Sun.

1. FIRST ROCKET

This was called a "fire-arrow," and was launched by an unknown Chinese inventor around 900 CE.

ITEMS LEFT ON THE MOON

Many spacecraft and 12 people have been to the Moon, and they have left all sorts of things behind! Some were too heavy to bring home, and others were left as mementos.

MANY MESSAGES

In 1969, Armstrong and Aldrin left a disc with messages from the leaders of 73 countries inscribed on it.

EARTH ROCK

A piece of lava from Devil's Lake, Oregon, USA, was taken to the Moon in 1971 by James Irwin.

TWO GOLF BALLS

Two golf balls were left on the Moon after being played with by astronaut Alan Shepard in 1971.

THE FALLEN ASTRONAUT

A sculpture which commemorates the men who had died as a result of their work on space exploration.

ALSEPs

Apollo Lunar Surface Experiments Packages were used to carry out measurements and experiments on the Moon by the Apollo missions.

SPACE MIRRORS

Retro reflectors, which measure distances from Earth, are the only devices on the Moon that still work.

APOLLO DESCENT STAGES

The Apollo astronauts arrived on the Moon in small spacecraft called Lunar Modules (LMs). The bottom halves were left behind when the rest of the craft took the astronauts away again.

APOLLO ASCENT STAGES

Once the Lunar Modules (LMs) had returned the astronauts to the orbiting Command and Service Modules, the LMs could fall back onto the Moon.

VINTAGE EXPLORER

The oldest man-made thing left on the Moon is the wreckage of *Luna 2*, a Russian moon probe which arrived in September 1959.

LUNAR ROVERS

Apollo missions 15, 16, and 17 all took electric cars called Lunar Rovers with them.

MOON CARS
The rovers allowed the astronauts to explore much farther than they could travel on foot.

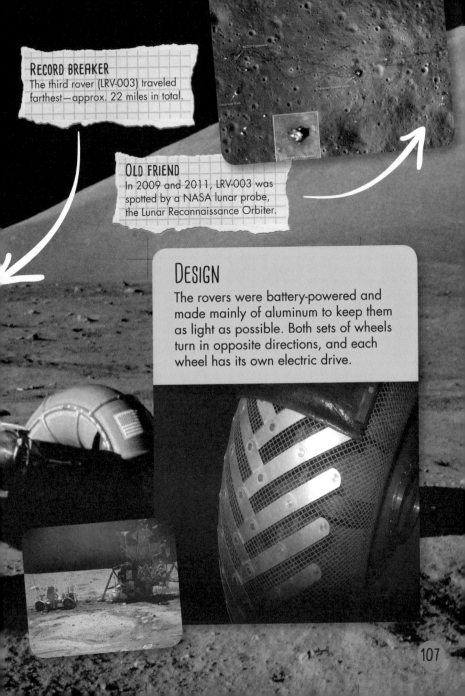

RECORD BREAKER
The third rover (LRV-003) traveled farthest—approx. 22 miles in total.

OLD FRIEND
In 2009 and 2011, LRV-003 was spotted by a NASA lunar probe, the Lunar Reconnaissance Orbiter.

DESIGN

The rovers were battery-powered and made mainly of aluminum to keep them as light as possible. Both sets of wheels turn in opposite directions, and each wheel has its own electric drive.

STRANGEST SPACE-TRAVELING OBJECTS

Although every extra pound of material sent into space increases the fuel and therefore the cost of the mission, astronauts are allowed to take small, light personal possessions with them. Many of which are very strange.

10. PIECES OF THE WRIGHT FLYER

Pieces of the first ever plane were sent on three separate missions—the first was the Apollo 11 moon-landing mission in 1969.

9. 398 POSTAL COVERS

Commemorative postal stamp covers were taken to the Moon by the crew of Apollo 15 to be sold back on Earth.

8. 400-YEAR-OLD CARGO TAG

Taken from Jamestown, the first European settlement in America.

7. GOLF CLUB

Alan Shepherd took one to the Moon in 1971 and played with it using two balls.

6. LEGO FIGURINES

Special Lego versions of Galileo and two Roman gods were onboard the Juno mission, launched in 2007.

5. LEGO BRICKS

Which were used to make a model of the ISS on the ISS in 2012.

4. ACTORS

Ashes of Star Trek creator Gene Roddenberry and James Doohan, who played Scotty, were both sent into space.

3. LUKE SKYWALKER'S LIGHTSABER

The original prop from the *Star Wars* movies was taken to the ISS in 2007.

2. BUZZ LIGHTYEAR

A figurine of the film character spent 15 months on the ISS.

1. TREE SEEDS

In 1971 the Apollo 14 mission took some tree seeds with it which were planted when they returned to Earth.

SPACE SELECTION
Five kinds of tree seeds were chosen—Douglas Fir, Loblolly Pine, Redwood, Sweetgum, and Sycamore.

MOON EXPERIMENT
The idea was to see if there was anything unusual about trees that grew from seeds that had been in space. Nothing unusual was found.

LOST FOREST
Although more than 400 "Moon trees" grew from the seeds, the locations of only a few dozen are now known.

"MOON TREES" ON EARTH
One seed was grown in Brazil and one in Italy. All the others were grown in the USA.

111

GREATEST ROCKET ENGINEERS AND SPACE SCIENTISTS

Space is studied in many ways—by working out its mathematical laws, by observing what it contains through telescopes, or by exploring it in spacecraft. The people who carry out these studies include some of the most brilliant who have ever lived.

10. STEPHEN HAWKING (BORN 1942)

Explained the science of black holes and helped develop new theories about the universe.

9. WERNHER VON BRAUN (1912–1977)

Rocket scientist who worked on V2 rockets in Germany and *Apollo* spacecraft in the USA.

8. SERGEY KOROLEV (1906–1966)

The Russian rocket designer who led the Soviet space program in the 1960s.

7. GEORGES LEMAITRE (1894–1966)

Devised the Big Bang theory of the beginning of the universe.

6. Edwin Hubble
(1889–1953)

Discovered that our galaxy is one of many and helped prove that the universe is expanding.

5. Robert Goddard
(1882–1945)

Launched the first liquid-fuel rocket in 1926.

4. Albert Einstein
(1879–1955)

Discovered how time, space, and gravity are related and how to figure out the shape of the universe.

3. Konstantin Tsiolkovsky
(1857–1935)

Russian developer of rocket theory and designer of spacecraft.

2. William Herschel
(1738–1822)

Discovered the planet Uranus and, with his sister Caroline (1750–1838), found many new comets.

1. ISAAC NEWTON
(1642–1727)

Isaac Newton was one of the greatest scientists to have ever lived, and his laws of gravitation and motion are still used to predict the positions of planets, moons, and comets and to figure out how to send spacecraft to their destinations. He also invented the reflecting telescope and calculus, used to calculate the paths of objects in space.

▶ **GREATEST SCIENTIST**
Newton was the greatest scientist of his time and perhaps the greatest ever.

▲ LAW OF GRAVITATION
Newton realized that gravity operated throughout the universe and devised an equation to calculate its strength.

SATELLITE INVENTOR
One of Newton's diagrams shows that if an object moves fast enough, it will go into orbit.

[13]

AXIOMATA
SIVE
LEGES MOTUS

Lex. I.

Corpus omne perseverare in statu suo quiescendi vel movendi uniformiter in directum, nisi quatenus a viribus impressis cogitur statum illum mutare.

Projectilia perseverant in motibus suis nisi quatenus a resistentia aeris retardantur & vi gravitatis impelluntur deorsum. Trochus, cujus partes cohaerendo perpetuo retrahunt sese a motibus rectilineis, non cessat rotari nisi quatenus ab aere retardatur. Majora autem Planetarum & Cometarum corpora motus suos & progressivos & circulares in spatiis minus resistentibus factos conservant diutius.

Lex. II.

Mutationem motus proportionalem esse vi motrici impressae, & fieri secundum lineam rectam qua vis illa imprimitur.

Si vis aliqua motum quemvis generet, dupla duplum, tripla triplum generabit, sive simul & semel, sive gradatim & successive impressa fuerit. Et hic motus quoniam in eandem semper plagam cum vi generatrice determinatur, si corpus antea movebatur, motui ejus vel conspiranti additur, vel contrario subducitur, vel obliquo oblique adjicitur, & cum eo secundum utriusque determinationem componitur.

Lex. II

▲ LAWS OF MOTION
Newton's three laws of motion are still used today to figure out how spacecraft will move.

MOST SURPRISING SPACE INVENTIONS

Space programs sometimes need better technology than what is available on Earth, so it has to be specially designed for them—and it often turns out to be useful in other ways too. Meanwhile, research on board space stations leads to major new breakthroughs.

10. BETTER WATER FILTERS

Water is heavy, so spacecraft cannot carry much. Instead, they use filter systems to clean and recycle it. The same systems are used to filter water on Earth.

9. PANORAMAS

Mars rovers took many separate pictures, and computer programs merged them into single large images (panoramas). The same software is now used in digital cameras.

8. BETTER SNEAKERS

The highest-quality sneakers use cushioning technology developed for space suits.

7. JOYSTICKS

For computer games, developed from similar instruments used to steer spacecraft.

6. Memory foam

Which returns to its original shape after being crushed.

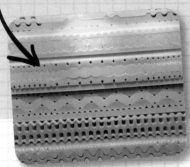

5. Better cans

In spacecraft, air-tight seals are essential. On Earth, soda cans and other containers use similar techniques.

4. Aluminium foil

Developed to wrap spacecraft like the *Lunar Module*.

3. Perfect chips

Better semiconductors for computer chips resulted from research into crystal growth carried out on the ISS.

2. Scratch-resistant lenses

Scratch-resistant lenses for glasses were invented thanks to a NASA scientist who developed a special clear plastic coating for space helmets. They were first sold in 1983.

1. SOLAR PANELS

Solar panels are used on many kinds of spacecraft to turn sunlight into electricity.

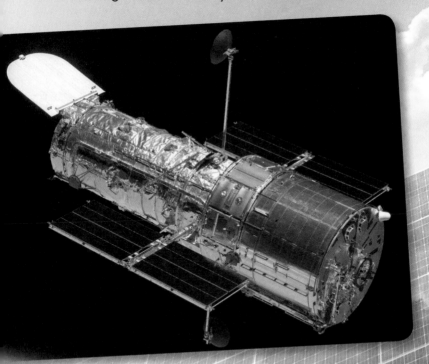

POWER FROM LIGHT
Light is a kind of energy, and when it falls on some metals and other substances this energy causes electricity to flow.

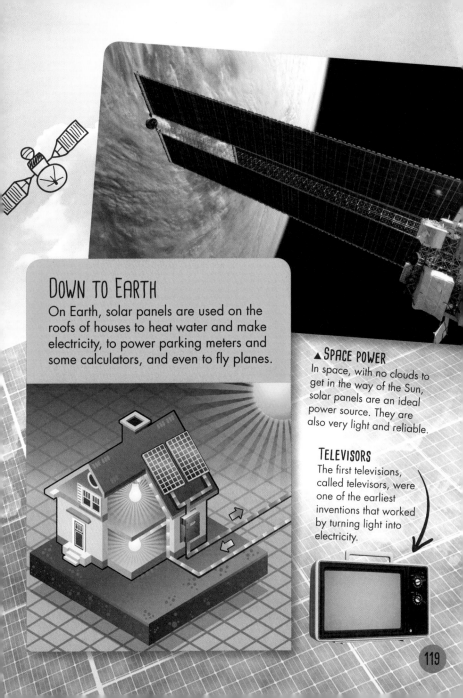

DOWN TO EARTH

On Earth, solar panels are used on the roofs of houses to heat water and make electricity, to power parking meters and some calculators, and even to fly planes.

▲ SPACE POWER

In space, with no clouds to get in the way of the Sun, solar panels are an ideal power source. They are also very light and reliable.

TELEVISORS

The first televisions, called televisors, were one of the earliest inventions that worked by turning light into electricity.

119

MARS EXPLORATION
REQUIREMENTS

When astronauts go to Mars, they will plan to stay there for several weeks. So they will need to make their home there, and they will have to use the resources of Mars itself to survive.

10. WATER

Some water will be collected from the air and soil, but most will be recycled.

9. SURVEY ROBOTS

Intelligent robots will crawl over the landscape, looking for signs of water and chemicals for fuel-making.

8. ROVERS

Electrically powered cars will be needed for long-range exploration.

7. SOLAR POWER ARRAYS

To provide power to the Mars base, extensive supplies of solar panels will be laid on the ground.

4. GARDEN

6. PRESSURE DOME

People cannot breathe the thin air on Mars, so they will need a pressurized habitat there.

It's possible that astronauts might take animals to Mars with them, and they will certainly take plants.

5. GYM

The low gravity on Mars could weaken bones and muscles, so keeping fit will be essential.

FRESH SCIENCE

Any differences between the way the Martian plants grow and their normal versions on Earth may help us learn about Mars and improve the growth of crops on Earth.

▼FRESH FOOD

Beans are quick and easy to grow, and are packed with vitamins too.

FRESH AIR

Plants produce oxygen, the gas we need to breathe. They also take in carbon dioxide, which we breathe out.

▲ FRESH AND FAMILIAR

Mars is a dead and dull-colored world. Colorful and fragrant plants will help the explorers to feel more at home there.

3. FUEL FACTORY

Spacecraft to Mars won't be powerful enough to take all the fuel they need to return to Earth. So fuel will be made on Mars.

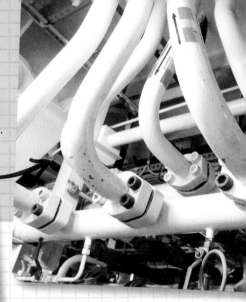

2. DIGGERS

Any signs of life on Mars will probably be underground, so special diggers will be used to search for it.

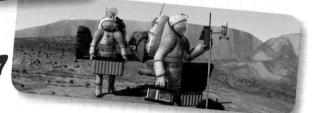

1. COMMUNICATION SYSTEMS

Powerful radio transmitters and sensitive receivers will keep astronauts in touch with Earth.

FUTURE SPACE GADGETS

Robots have been very successful in exploring the solar system, and many new kinds are being developed. For astronauts, future space exploration will involve much longer journeys, and new technology will be needed if they are to survive them.

10. CRYOGENIC MODULES

For long journeys, astronauts may "hibernate" for months in chilled cabinets.

9. ROBONAUTS

Human-shaped robots will assist astronauts in dangerous tasks.

8. INSPECTION ROBOTS

Small hovering robots will move around outside the spacecraft, checking for damage and making simple repairs.

7. INFLATABLE SPACE STATIONS

Experimental modules that unfold in space have already been built. Space stations built in this way would be easier to launch to orbit and could be adapted to the number of astronauts on board.

6. REUSABLE CRAFT

SPACE SHUTTLE
The NASA space shuttle was largely reusable. Although its boosters were discarded after launch, some were collected and refilled.

Spacecraft are extremely expensive to build, yet most can only be used once. The ideal would be a craft that could be used over and over again.

United States

Discovery

BURAN REUSABLE SHUTTLE

A Russian reusable space shuttle was built in the 1980s, but never used.

RETURNABLE STAGES

Instead of simply dropping rocket stages to burn up in the atmosphere or sink into the sea, it may be possible to fit small thrusters to them, so that they can fly back to their launch site.

▶ SSTOs

New light materials may soon make it possible to reach orbit without discarding rocket stages on the way. Such vehicles are called Single Stage to Orbit (SSTO) spacecraft.

5. Super 3D printers

Explorers of distant worlds may not know what tools they need until they get there. Instead, mission control on Earth could send instructions to an onboard printer to produce them to order.

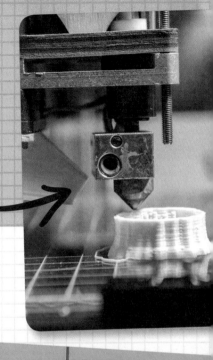

4. Melt mirrors

Also known as Transformers, melt mirrors would use reflected sunlight to melt tunnels in the icy surfaces of frozen moons to explore them and to provide drinking water.

3. Tensegrity robots

Small robots made mainly of jointed rods, tensegrity robots could be dropped on many planets and moons and left to explore them.

2. Cubecraft

Tiny cubical spacecraft, 4 inches long, could explore the solar system quickly and inexpensively.

1. Maneuvering Units

To move freely in space, astronauts will need improved jet-powered systems.

GREATEST THREATS FROM SPACE

The Earth can't always protect us from dangers from beyond. Some of these dangers already cause death and damage on Earth, and others devastated our planet long ago. Some, though unlikely to happen, could destroy the world if they did.

10. GALAXY COLLISION

Our galaxy (the Milky Way) is on a collision course with the huge Andromeda Galaxy. But the collision won't happen for millions of years, and even then the Earth will probably be undamaged.

9. ALIEN INVASIONS

Human beings have been sending radio signals out to space for decades. There has been no reply, but if anyone—or anything—has received them, they will know exactly where to find us.

8. BLACK HOLES

Black holes destroy everything near them. It is just possible that a small one could drift through space and destroy the Earth.

7. SPACE PLAGUES

Some scientists think life was brought to the Earth by comets. A few believe a future comet might possibly bring alien bacteria or viruses.

6. DARK CLOUDS

There are many dark dust clouds in space, and if one drifted between us and the Sun, the Earth would freeze. But we would be able to see the cloud many years before it arrived.

5. METEORITES

Although there have been near misses, no one has been known to be killed by a meteorite, so they are a slight, but real, risk.

4. ASTEROIDS

The dinosaurs were wiped out by an asteroid (or perhaps a comet) that struck the Earth 66 million years ago. There have been many other such "mass extinctions," and there are more to come.

3. SOLAR SHIFTS

In the sixteenth century, the Earth became much colder than usual, perhaps because the Sun gave out less energy for a while. A larger shift like this could either freeze or bake our world.

2. SPACE RADIATION

Many people die each year from skin cancer, caused by the Sun. The atmosphere's ozone layer protects us to an extent from the Sun, but it is very vulnerable to some pollutants.

1. Geomagnetic storm

The Sun constantly sends tiny particles out into space, and when there is an especially strong burst of them, they can block or interfere with phone calls, TV broadcasts, and even power supplies on Earth.

Blackout

Storms can generate electrical pulses inside power cables, causing widespread power cuts.

RADIO SILENCE

Communication satellites are sometimes dislodged, cutting off TV, radio, and some phone signals.

STORM WARNINGS

When the solar wind is unusually powerful, astronomers know that it will affect the Earth's magnetic field, causing electrical disturbances in our atmosphere.

DISCONNECTED

Cables carrying phone and internet links can be interrupted, even those deep underwater.

BRIGHTEST STARS

About two thousand years ago, the Greek astronomer Hipparchus grouped the stars into six "magnitude" groups according to their brightness. The brightest stars had a magnitude of 1. We still use a similar system today, although now the brightest stars have magnitudes of less than 1.

10. ACHERNAR
(MAGNITUDE 0.50)
16% as bright as the star Sirius.

9. BETELGEUSE
(MAGNITUDE 0.42)
18% as bright as Sirius.

8. PROCYON
(MAGNITUDE 0.34)
19% as bright as Sirius.

7. RIGEL
(MAGNITUDE 0.12)
23% as bright as Sirius.

6. CAPELLA
(MAGNITUDE 0.08)
Just less than a quarter as bright as Sirius.

5. VEGA
(MAGNITUDE 0.03)
One quarter as bright as Sirius.

4. ARCTURUS
(MAGNITUDE -0.04)
Just over a quarter as bright as Sirius.

3. ALPHA CENTAURI
(MAGNITUDE -0.27)
One third as bright as Sirius.

2. CANOPUS
(MAGNITUDE -0.72)
About half as bright as Sirius.

1. SIRIUS

By far the brightest star in the night sky, Sirius (magnitude -1.46) is also one of the most famous.

DOG STAR

Many ancient civilizations referred to Sirius as the Dog Star.

CALENDAR STAR

The ancient Egyptians had a calendar based on the appearances of Sirius.

▲ SYSTEM STAR
Through a telescope it is clear that Sirius is actually a pair of stars, with one much brighter than the other.

GUIDE STAR
Polynesian sailors used the position of Sirius to steer by.

CLOSEST STARS

If the stars were all the same, then the closest ones would look the brightest. But actually the true brightness (luminosity) of one star is often very different from another. If you compare this list with the one on brightest stars, you will see that only two stars are in both lists. Distances are given in light years—one light year is roughly 6 trillion miles.

10. LACILLE 9352
(10.7 LIGHT YEARS AWAY)

An unusually bright red star, bright enough to be seen with binoculars.

9. EPSILON ERIDANI
(10.5 LIGHT YEARS AWAY)

Has a planet the size of Jupiter orbiting it.

8. ROSS 248
(10.3 LIGHT YEARS AWAY)

There are several "Ross" stars, so called because they were cataloged by astronomer Frank Elmore Ross in 1926.

7. ROSS 154
(9.6 LIGHT YEARS AWAY)

Flares up, every 2 Earth days or so.

6. UV CETI A
(8.9 LIGHT YEARS AWAY)

Produces enormous flares of light.

5. Sirius A and B
(8.6 light years away)

Sirius B is a very tiny star called a white dwarf, which is the glowing core that is all that remains of a long-dead star.

4. Lalande 21185
(8.29 light years away)

A very red and very ancient star; perhaps 10 billion years old, which is more than twice as old as the Sun.

3. Wolf 359
(7.7 light years away)

So dim that it was only discovered in 1916, despite being a close neighbor.

2. Barnard's Star
(6.0 light years away)

Once thought likely to have a habitable planet, Barnard's Star was an early target for planned interstellar missions.

1. PROXIMA CENTAURI

Other than the Sun, Proxima Centauri is the closest star to us (4.2 light years away).

MULTIPLE STAR
Proxima Centauri is one of a group of stars, which we see as a single star, called Alpha Centauri.

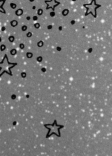

DISTANT STAR

Even Proxima Centauri is a long way away—more than a quarter of a million times farther than the Sun.

▲ PLANETS?

It is thought that Proxima Centauri may have at least one planet, located about half as far from it as the Earth is from the Sun.

▼ APPROACH TO EARTH

Proxima Centauri is moving toward us at approximately 13 miles per second. It will be at its closest in 26,700 years, when it will pass us at a distance of 3.11 light years.

THE SUN'S CLOSEST NEIGHBORS

WISE 0855-0714
(distance 2014)

6 LIGHT YEARS

WISE 1049-5319
(distance 2013)

Barnard's Star
(distance 1916)

4 LIGHT YEARS

Alpha Centauri
(distance 1839)

Proxima Centauri
(distance 1917)

2 LIGHT YEARS

SUN

MOST EXTREME STARS

It is not only in brightness that stars differ from each other. They also vary widely in color, mass, size, and many other measures. Some of these characteristics go together—massive stars are usually bright, and large ones are usually red.

10. BRIGHTEST EXPLODING STAR

Supernova SN1006 was first seen in 1006 and is bright enough to be seen in daytime.

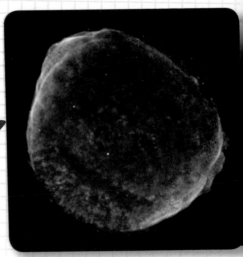

9. FASTEST

Barnard's Star, which moves across the sky at 10.3 arcseconds per year, is the fastest (though it would still take two centuries for it to move the width of the Moon).

8. MOST PLANETS

HD 10180, which has the most planets, with nine.

7. R136a1

A monster among stars, R136a1 is much too far away to see with the naked eye.

▼ **HOTTEST STAR**
(89,500°F) The Sun is only 9,941°F.

UNBEATABLE STAR?

Astronomers think that R136a1 is just about as hot and bright as any star can be without destroying itself.

▲BRIGHTEST STAR

7.4 million times brighter than the Sun.

MOST MASSIVE STAR

265 times bigger than the Sun.

6. Bluest

The bluest star is Eta Carinae (actually a pair of stars).

5. Reddest

Mu Cephei is the reddest star (also called Herschel's Garnet Star).

4. Oldest

HD 140283, the Methuselah star, is more than 13 billion years old (about 3 times as old as the Sun).

3. Coldest

CFBDSIR 1458+10B is the coldest star at around 212°F.

2. Smallest

2MASS J05233822-1403022 is the smallest star, with a radius of about 8.6% of that of the Sun.

1. Biggest

The biggest star is UY Scuti, a red star about 1,710 times as wide as the Sun.

NEXT MAJOR SPACE PROJECTS

Most major missions in the next few decades will be to the planet Mars. After that, there will be many voyages through the solar system, and far in the future the exploration of the stars will begin.

10. HUMANS TO EXOPLANETS

If we can invent systems to allow astronauts to hibernate for centuries, huge spacecraft could ferry them to exoplanets (3000s?).

9. TERRAFORMING MARS

By planting special crops and reflecting sunlight onto Mars, it may be possible to transform it into our second home (2500s?).

8. ROBOTS TO EXOPLANETS

The huge distances to stars mean long journeys. The first probes will probably weigh just a few ounces and take about 50 years to get there (2060s?).

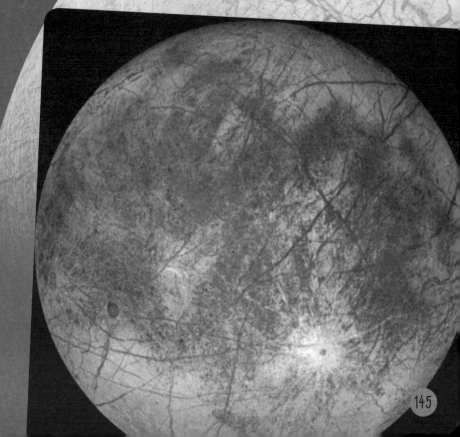

7. EUROPA MISSION

LIFE IN THE DARK
We know that life exists in the black, cold depths of our own oceans. It might exist in Europa's oceans too.

Europa, a moon of Jupiter, has a warm underground ocean which scientists would love to explore (2040s?).

145

EUROPA CONT.

GRAVITY POWER

Europa is so close to Jupiter that the giant planet's gravity pulls and pushes at its interior, warming it up and keeping the water from freezing.

MELTING ICE

To get through the thick layer of ice that caps the ocean, reflected sunlight will be focused on it.

▶ UNDER THE SURFACE

A robotic submarine will explore the ocean, sending information back by a cable and maybe catching swimming creatures too.

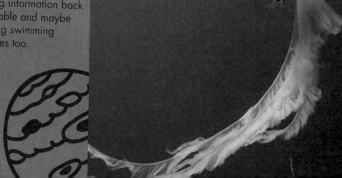

6. Asteroid Mining

Some asteroids are rich in valuable metals and could be moved closer to Earth to be mined (2040s?).

4. OPSEK
(Orbital Piloted Assembly and Experiment Complex)

This will be a Russian space station recycled from parts of the ISS when it is shut down sometime in the late 2020s.

3. Inspiration Mars

A proposed mission to send two astronauts around Mars and back to Earth (2025).

2. Mars 2020

Unlike previous rovers, *Mars 2020* will be able to send samples back to Earth (2020).

5. Crewed Mars Mission

A crewed mission to Mars has been on the agenda since 1969, but it will be so expensive that we don't know when it will happen (2030s?).

1. Private Spaceplanes

Anyone with enough money will be able to travel into space (this is being developed now).

MOST IMPORTANT VARIABLE STARS

Although the stars look the same to us each time we see them, many of them change in brightness over periods of years, hours, or even seconds. The study of variable stars has taught astronomers a lot about how all stars work.

10. SPOTTED STAR

Enormous dark spots make these stars look dim, then bright again at the spot.

9. R CORONAE BOREALIS (RCB) STAR

Huge soot clouds block out the light from these stars.

8. FLARE STAR

These stars flare like the Sun, but much more brightly.

7. NOVA

A star that explodes over and over again.

6. MIRA

The earliest variable star to be discovered, in 1596. Its name means "the wonderful."

5. ALGOL

Its name means "the Ghoul," and it is also known as the demon star.

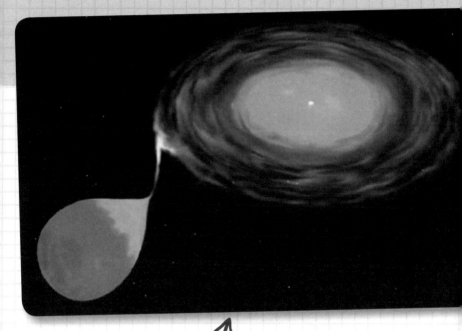

4. PULSAR

A tiny, fast-spinning star that we detect by its radio signals.

2. SUPERNOVA

The brightest of all variables, a supernova can outshine a whole galaxy.

3. ECLIPSING BINARY

When one star gets in front of a partner star, the ways in which the light changes tell us a lot about both stars.

1. CEPHEID

Cepheid variable stars are by far the most useful kind of variable stars—astronomers use them to map out the universe.

▼ OLD FAITHFUL

Cepheids constantly pulse in and out, getting bright and hot, then dim and cool as they do so. The changes are extremely regular.

▶ BRIGHTNESS TO DISTANCE

By comparing the known brightness of a Cepheid with how bright it looks, astronomers can figure out how far away it is. So, Cepheids can be used to measure out the universe.

DISCOVERY

The first Cepheid was discovered by John Goodricke in 1754. It had a period of 6 years.

▶ PULSATION EQUATION

In 1908, Henrietta Swan Leavitt found that brighter Cepheids pulsate faster, so she could figure out the brightness of a Cepheid from its pulsation rate.

151

STRANGEST STARS

Most of the stars we can see are glowing balls of hydrogen gas. Most are larger than the Sun but otherwise similar. However, some stars are very different, and a few are quite weird indeed.

10. MAGNETARS

An intensely magnetic kind of neutron star, a magnetar sends powerful bursts of x-rays and gamma rays out into space.

9. BLACK DWARFS

Many stars leave behind glowing cores called white dwarfs. When these have completely cooled, they will form black dwarfs. But the cooling is so slow that there are no black dwarfs in the universe yet.

8. WOLF–RAYET STARS

These are extremely hot stars with powerful winds of particles blowing from them which shine brightly in ultraviolet light.

7. RV TAURI STARS

Many stars change in size, but RV Tauri stars change in shape too, from that of grapefruits to rugby balls.

6. Thorne–Żytkow Objects

When a neutron star collides with a red giant star, it can remain stuck deep inside. Just one such merged star is known, called HV 2112.

5. Quark Stars

These super-dense stars made of quarks are not known for sure to exist. Usually quarks are locked up inside atoms.

4. Neutron Stars

Stars so crushed that the material they are made of is like the core of an atom.

3. Contact Binaries

Pairs of stars so close to each other that they touch.

2. Black Holes

Super-dense stars that draw in everything nearby.

1. QUASARS

Some of the brightest and most distant objects in the universe are quasars.

▶ ANCIENT LIGHT
There are no quasars anymore. The ones we see were so far away that their light is still reaching us, billions of years after it left them.

▼ GALAXY CORES
Quasars are the brightly glowing cores of distant galaxies.

The first quasar, called 3C 273, was discovered in 1959. Its radio emissions were detected before it was seen.

QUASAR POWER
The bright light and powerful radio emissions are powered by material falling into a black hole.

Oddest BLACK HOLE Facts

When enough matter is squeezed into a small enough space, gravity becomes so intense that the object collapses in on itself, forming a black hole.

10. White Holes?

Some scientists think that all the matter that falls into a black hole bursts out of a white hole in another part of the universe.

9. Shortcuts

Black holes may cause the formation of narrow corridors through space, linking distant regions of the universe.

8. Back to the Start

Spinning black holes may allow astronauts to travel back in time to when they first formed.

7. Black Explosions

Stephen Hawking showed that large black holes will eventually explode.

6. BLACK CENTER

Our galaxy has an enormous black hole at its core.

5. SINGULARITY

In the center of a black hole lurks a singularity, where the laws of our universe no longer apply.

4. SPAGHETTIFIED

Very close to a black hole, the gravity would pull much harder on your feet than your head—stretching you out like a piece of spaghetti.

3. SLOW TIME

Black hole gravity slows down time. Gravity is so strong near a black hole that the flow of time slows down massively compared to the flow of time far away from the hole, on Earth.

2. NO ESCAPE

The gravity of a black hole is so powerful that not even light can escape—which is why black holes are black.

157

1. STRANGE NEIGHBOR

Cygnus X-1 is the closest black hole to us and the first to be discovered.

In 1971, Cygnus X-1 was discovered to be a strong source of radio waves when it was studied by the Westerbork array of radio telescopes.

UHURU

An X-ray astronomy satellite, Uhuru was launched in 1970 mainly to study Cygnus X-1.

BINARY

The signals were tracked down to a blue supergiant star in orbit around an invisible companion—a black hole.

STRANGE RAYS

The X-rays from Cygnus X-1 were first detected by an unmanned spacecraft in 1964, long before the star itself was found.

RECORD-BREAKING EXOPLANETS

An exoplanet is a planet that goes around a star other than the Sun, and hundreds are now known. An exoplanet is usually found because when it passes in front of its parent star, it blocks out some of the star's light.

10. SHORTEST YEAR

Kepler 78-b has the shortest year, lasting just 5.6 hours.

9. LONGEST YEAR

GU Piscium B has the longest year, lasting 163,000 years.

8. COLDEST

OGLE-2005-BLG-390L b is the coldest known exoplanet with a temperature of around −370°F.

7. HOTTEST

Kepler 78b is the hottest exoplanet at 5,119°F—hot enough to melt iron.

6. SMALLEST

Kepler 37-b is the smallest exoplanet, about the size of our Moon.

5. LARGEST

HAT-P-32b is the largest exoplanet—twice the size of Jupiter.

3. CLOSEST

Alpha Centauri Bb is just 4.37 light years away.

4. FARTHEST

OGLE-2005-BLG-390L is 21,500 light years away.

2. FIRST

The first (and second) exoplanets were proved to exist in 1992 (there had been signs of them for some years before). Along with a third, discovered in 1994, they are in orbit around a pulsar about 1,000 light years from Earth, called PSR B1257+12.

1. MOST EARTH-LIKE

Kepler 438 b. The Kepler satellite is designed to find exoplanets, so many have names that begin with "Kepler."

GOLDILOCKS WORLD

For a planet to support life it must be in an area of space around a star called the Goldilocks zone, which is not so hot that water boils away, nor so cold that it freezes.

EARTH-SIZED

Kepler 438 b is about 12% larger than Earth.

ROCK WORLD

Most exoplanets are gassy, like Jupiter. Kepler 438 b is rocky, like Earth.

MISSION TO KEPLER

The planet is about 470 light years away, more than a hundred times farther than the nearest star to us. So we will probably not be able to go there for thousands of years.

MOST EXTREME PLANETARY WEATHER

On Earth, bad weather is usually more inconvenient than dangerous, but many other worlds experience weather conditions so extreme that it would be almost impossible to survive them.

10. SUPERWINDS

The wind on Neptune can blow at over 1,242 miles an hour. On Earth, winds faster than 62 miles per hour are rare.

9. LIGHTNING STORMS

The lightning on Saturn is about 1,000 times more powerful than on Earth.

8. WORLDWIDE DUST

Mars has dust storms that last for months and cover the whole planet.

7. ELECTRIC SKIES

Exoplanet Gliese 1214 b is so hot that its atmosphere is made of electrical particles called electrons and ions.

6. LAVA FLOODS

Jupiter's moon, Io, is so hot that lava often surges over huge areas, as shown in this illustration.

5. Acid rain

The clouds of Venus rain sulfuric acid, which boils away before reaching the ground.

4. Boiling sunrise

When the Sun rises on Mercury, the temperature changes from colder than a freezer to hotter than an oven.

3. Metal rain

On exoplanet Luhman 16B, the rain is made of molten iron.

2. Falling sky

On Pluto, the atmosphere probably freezes in winter and falls to the ground like snow.

1. SUPERSTORM

Jupiter's Great Red Spot is a hurricane three times bigger than the Earth.

PIONEER DISCOVERY

The Spot was proven to definitely be a hurricane by the *Pioneer 10* probe in 1973.

VINTAGE STORM
The Spot was first seen in 1635 and has remained ever since.

AGE SECRET
The Spot has lasted so long because it is so big, making it very stable. Smaller spots often come and go on Jupiter.

◄ COLOR STORM
The Spot is red because it drags up gases from deep down in Jupiter's atmosphere.

MOST AMAZING THINGS TO SEE IN THE NIGHT SKY WITHOUT A TELESCOPE

Most of the images in this book were taken by enormous telescopes or by satellites. But amazing things can be seen with the naked eye, especially if you can get far enough away from city lights.

10. MARS

Mars is bright and red, and can be seen every two years.

9. JUPITER

The brightest midnight planet at certain times of year—check the NASA website for details.

8. THE ANDROMEDA GALAXY

This can be seen in the Northern Hemisphere, or in the Southern Hemisphere you can see the Magellanic clouds. You'll need very dark conditions though.

7. ISS

The high speed and large size of the ISS make it easy to spot if you use the internet to tell you where to look.

6. ORION NEBULA

This looks like a glowing cloud, just below Orion's belt.

5. VENUS

Often visible in the west (the direction of the setting Sun) soon after sunset.

4. PLEIADES

Also known as Seven Sisters, is a nearby "open" star cluster.

3. LUNAR SEAS

The dark patches on the Moon are visible even from brightly lit cities.

2. LUNAR ECLIPSES

There is usually at least one lunar eclipse a year, and it turns the Moon blood-red.

1. METEORS

When grit and stones from space fall through our atmosphere, they appear as streaks of light called meteors or shooting stars.

► WHEN?
Most meteors appear in showers. The best is the Perseid shower, from mid-July to mid-August.

AUGUST
8

WHERE?
From the direction of the constellation of Perseus.

WHAT TIME?
After midnight on a moonless night.

▲ HOW?
Lie on a sleeping bag on the ground, look up, and wait.

MOST **VISIBLE** CONSTELLATIONS

Since ancient times, people have connected the stars to make patterns that remind them of animals and other things. The brightest constellations were defined by the ancient Greeks. Others were added later, and there are now 88 of them.

10. LYRA
The lyre.

9. GEMINI
The twins.

8. SCORPIO
The scorpion.

7. TAURUS
The bull.

6. URSA MINOR

The little bear (best seen from the Northern Hemisphere).

5. LEO

The lion.

4. CYGNUS

The swan.

3. CASSIOPEIA

The mythical wife of the king of ancient Ethiopia (best seen from the Northern Hemisphere).

2. URSA MAJOR

The great bear (best seen from the Northern Hemisphere).

1. ORION

The Hunter is one of the most recognizable of all constellations, and there are pictures and carvings of it from many ancient civilizations. The earliest is about 35,000 years old.

SWORD
Three stars form Orion's sword, together with the Orion nebula.

MAIN STARS
His shoulders are Betelgeuse and Bellatrix, and his knees are Saiph and Rigel.

ORION
The oldest known human carving thought to be of Orion is a very small ivory plate with a human figure engraving on one side and what is thought to be a star chart on the other side. It is 35,000 years old.

BELT
The three bright stars Alnitak, Alnilam, and Mintaka are lined up to form his belt.

WEIRDEST SKY PHENOMENA

There is plenty more to see in the sky than stars and planets. Strange glows and flashes appear both by day and night. Most are due to the effects of our own atmosphere.

10. ZODIACAL LIGHT

This is a dim, cone-shaped glow caused by sunlit interplanetary dust.

9. SUNDOGS AND MOONDOGS

Rainbow patches left and right of the Sun or Moon, caused by ice crystals.

8. RINGS AROUND THE MOON

These are caused by ice crystals in the sky.

7. NOCTILUCENT CLOUDS

These are glowing clouds in twilight skies, lit by the Sun after it has set.

6. MOONBOWS

These are made from moonlight and raindrops.

5. GREEN FLASH

A very rare and brief green glow as the Sun sets.

4. GLORIES

Rainbow-colored halos caused by sunlit water droplets.

3. FIREBALLS

Enormous, colorful meteors.

2. CREPUSCULAR RAYS

These are made by sunbeams shining through cloud gaps.

1. AURORA BOREALIS AND AUSTRALIS

The Northern Lights and Southern Lights are probably the most beautiful things in the sky.

WHERE TO SEE THEM
From as close to the north or south pole as possible.

WHEN TO SEE THEM
In the winter. They are brightest every eleven years.

► **WHAT YOU'RE SEEING**
The effects of the wind colliding with Earth's magnetic field.

HOW THEY LOOK FROM SPACE

They look even more amazing from space!

179

MOST IMPORTANT TELESCOPES AND OBSERVATORIES

10. Advance Laser Interferometer Gravitational Wave Observatory (Advanced LIGO)

A new telescope to detect gravity waves from objects moving in space.

9. Kuiper Airborne Observatory

A flying observatory that rises above the thickest parts of our atmosphere to see rays that the air usually blocks.

8. Super-Kamiokande Neutrino Telescope (Super-K)

Buried deep underground under Mount Kamioka near the city of Hida, Japan, Super-K detects particles called neutrinos from the Sun and beyond.

7. Nuclear Spectroscopic Telescope Array (NuStar)

X-ray space telescope, exploring some of the most violent events in the universe.

6. Low-Frequency Array for Radio Astronomy (LOFAR)

The biggest network of separate radio telescopes, which works as one single enormous one.

5. Spectroscopic Planet Observatory for Recognition of Interaction of Atmosphere (SPRINT-A)

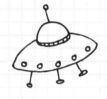

An advanced ultraviolet space telescope, also called Hisaki.

4. Fermi Gamma-Ray Space Telescope

Orbiting telescope that studies the most powerful radiation there is.

3. Arecibo Radio Telescope

The world's biggest radio telescope dish, in Puerto Rico, used partly to search for alien life.

181

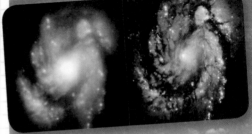

DESIGN
As well as making images from visible light, the HST is sensitive to ultraviolet and infrared too.

2. EUROPEAN EXTREMELY LARGE TELESCOPE
(E-ELT).

Now under development, the E-ELT will be the most powerful telescope ever.

▲ **BLURRED VISION**
The first images from the HST, received in 1990, were blurry and almost useless.

1. HUBBLE SPACE TELESCOPE (HST)

From its orbit high above Earth, the Hubble Space Telescope has sent back the most amazing images and helped to make many new discoveries.

▼ DEEP FIELD
The deep field is one of the HST's most famous images, showing the distant universe.

▲ REPAIR

An emergency mission by space shuttle was quickly arranged to repair the HST.

MOST BEAUTIFUL NEBULAE

"Nebula" means cloud, and most nebulae really are clouds of dust or gas. In the eighteenth century, Charles Messier made a catalog of those he knew, so the brightest nebulae have "M" (for Messier) numbers as well as names.

10. TARANTULA

A cloud of glowing gas 160,000 light years away.

9. PILLARS OF CREATION

Shaped by the radiation of young stars, new stars are forming inside.

8. ORION

The brightest nebula in our sky and a birthplace of new stars.

7. HORSEHEAD

A nebula made of dust, seen against a glowing background of gas heated by a very hot star.

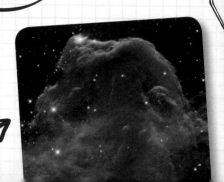

6. HELIX

A planetary nebula, photographed here in infrared light.

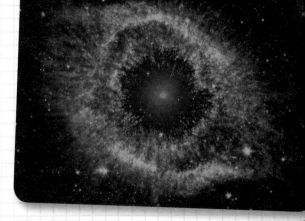

5. FLAMING STAR

Some of its light comes from glowing gas, while some is reflected from stars.

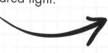

4. EMBRYO (SOUL)

Nebula in which new stars are being born.

3. CRAB

The remains of a supernova that exploded in 1054 CE.

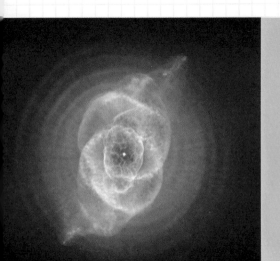

2. CAT'S EYE

A bright planetary nebula. Studies of the Cat's Eye in 1864 proved that planetary nebulae are clouds in space.

1. THE HOURGLASS NEBULA

The Hourglass Nebula is a planetary nebula made of the dust and gas that remain from an exploded star.

WHAT?
The white dot near the center is the white dwarf which was the core of the star that exploded to form the nebula.

WHERE?
The Hourglass is 8,000 light years away in the tiny constellation of Musca, the fly.

WHY?
The unusual double shape might be caused by an invisible cloud around it. The thicker parts of the cloud near the "waist" of the nebula might have held back its expansion there.

WHEN?
The nebula formed about 2,400 years ago, making it fairly young. It will fade away in a few thousand years.

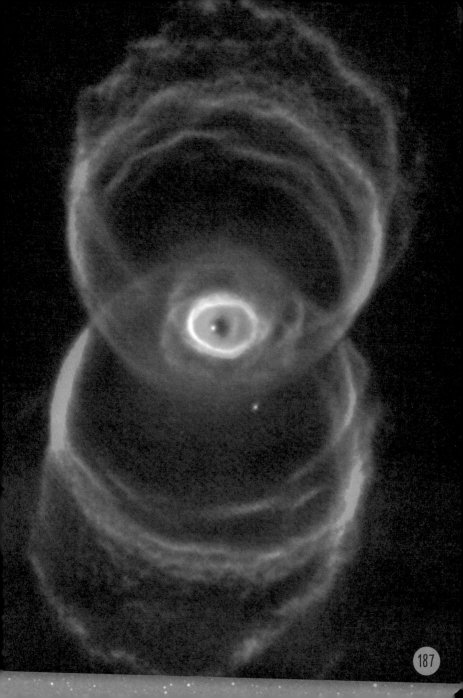

MOST SPECTACULAR
GALAXIES

A galaxy is a vast collection of stars. Galaxies are grouped together as clusters. Our galaxy is part of the cluster called the Local Group, of which M31 is also a member, and the clusters are grouped into superclusters. The Local Group is part of the Virgo supercluster.

10. NGC 660

A rare type of galaxy known as a polar ring galaxy. NGC 660 probably stole dust and gas from a passing galaxy long ago to develop its strange shape.

9. NGC 474

NGC stands for "New General Catalogue." NGC 474's rings may be the remains of old galaxies that it has drawn in.

8. BLACK EYE

Probably the result of the merging of two older galaxies, the red color at the center suggests many new stars are forming there.

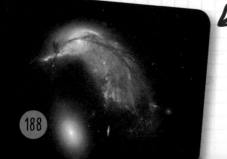

7. PORPOISE

This used to be a normal spiral galaxy, but the gravity of the egg-shaped galaxy below it has twisted the Porpoise into its current shape.

6. SOMBRERO (M104)

A spiral galaxy seen edge-on. The dark rim is made of dust clouds.

5. HOAG'S OBJECT

Mysterious ring galaxy named after Arthur Hoag, who discovered it in 1950.

3. PINWHEEL (M101)

The Pinwheel was discovered in 1781, and is 21 million light years away.

4. MICE

A pair of galaxies in the process of merging into one.

2. ANDROMEDA GALAXY (M31)

A spiral galaxy quite close to our own. It contains about one trillion stars—many more stars than there are in our own galaxy.

1. MILKY WAY

The Milky Way is our own galaxy, which looks like a long smear of milk across the night sky.

SEEING THE GALAXY
From our viewpoint inside the Milky Way, we see it as a band of misty light arching across in the night sky. Dark areas within it are dust clouds.

HOME IN SPACE
We are in one of the arms of the Milky Way, which is a spiral galaxy.

THE NEIGHBORHOOD

On a very clear night, you can see about 2,000 stars with the naked eye. This is less than 1% of all the stars in our galaxy.

SIZE

The Milky Way is larger than most galaxies. It is at least 100,000 light years across, contains more than 100 billion stars, and probably more than 100 billion planets.

▼ MAGELLANIC CLOUDS

From the Southern Hemisphere you can see two glowing masses of stars near the Milky Way. These are small separate galaxies called the Large and Small Magellanic clouds.

ANCIENT CREATION MYTHS

People have always wondered how the world began and where man came from. Until science developed answers for these, they made up stories called creation myths.

ODIN
The son and murderer of Ymir.

AZTEC
The goddess Coatlicue gave birth to the Moon and stars.

LOKI
Shape-changing enemy of Thor.

VIKING

THOR
Storm-god and son of Odin.

The Earth formed from the body of a giant, Ymir.

MUSPELL AND NIFLHEIM
Lands of fire and ice that existed before the Earth.

CHINESE

The world formed from a cosmic egg together with the body of Pan-gu, who emerged from the egg.

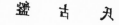

PERSIAN

The god Ahura Mazda created the world, beginning with Alburz, a mountain.

JAPANESE

The gods created a brother and sister who made land appear from the ocean.

GREEK

The first gods, including the Earth god Gaia, emerged from chaos and created the other gods and the world.

194

ISRAELI

God created the universe and everything in it in seven days, starting with light.

INDIAN

The giant Purusha was killed by the gods and his body formed the world.

EGYPTIAN

The world was just water until the god Atum created himself and then land.

BABYLONIAN

Apsu (god of fresh water) and Tiamat (god of salt water), created the other gods, and Tiamat's body became the Earth and sky.

195

MOST DRAMATIC MOMENTS IN TIME

By applying their knowledge of physics, mathematics, and chemistry to observations of the night sky and studies of the Earth, scientists in the twentieth century discovered how the universe, the Earth, and life began and developed.

BIG CHILL
All stars burn out and die, and the universe grows cold.

10. UNIVERSE ENDS?

The date of this possible event is unknown, and the details are uncertain.

BIG RIP
Galaxies, then stars, then planets, then atoms, then parts of atoms, tear themselves apart.

BIG CRUNCH
The universe collapses in on itself.

◀ BIG BOUNCE
The universe collapses in on itself and then explodes in a new Big Bang.

9. THE SUN DESTROYS US?

The Sun may become a red giant and destroy the Earth (about 5 billion years in the future).

8. LIFE EVOLVES

Life evolved on Earth about 3.9 billion years ago.

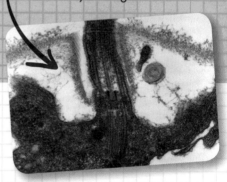

7. EARTH FORMS

The Earth formed 5.54 billion years ago.

6. SUN FORMS

The Sun formed 4.6 billion years ago, which is 9.2 billion years after the Big Bang.

5. FIRST STARS

The first stars formed about 500 million years after the Big Bang.

4. SPACE

Space became transparent 377,000 years after the Big Bang. Before that it was opaque, and light could not travel through it.

2. COSMIC INFLATION

A fraction of a second after the Big Bang, there was a short, sharp surge in size.

3. MATTER

Formed within 1 second of the Big Bang.

1. Big Bang

The universe began in the form of a tiny, very rapidly expanding point which was unimaginably hot and dense. This was 13.8 billion years ago.

MOST BAFFLING SPACE MYSTERIES

Although we now know an enormous amount about the planets, stars, and galaxies around us, and about the universe itself, many mysteries remain. Perhaps you will help to find the answers one day.

10. RADIO SOURCE SHGB02+14A

Radio source SHGB02+14A just might be an alien message.

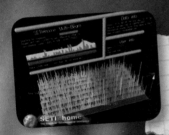

▲ DETECTION
The signal was found by the SETI@home project (left), which uses the power of the computers of volunteers all over the world to analyze radio telescope signals.

▼ WATER ALERT

The frequency of the signal is related to water. As any living thing needs water, it has been suggested that the use of this frequency is a way for aliens to signal their presence.

▼ SIGNAL CHECK

The Arecibo radio telescope, Puerto Rico (below) was used to confirm that the signal was real.

▼ SIGNAL FROM NOWHERE

The signal came from between the constellations of Aries and Pisces, where there are no known nearby stars.

9. THE WOW SIGNAL

A mysterious radio burst received in 1977 at a radio telescope in Ohio that came from nowhere on Earth.

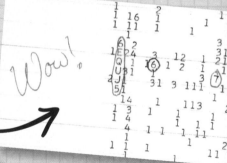

8. EARTH BOOST

When the Galileo Jupiter probe (left) passed the Earth in 1990, it suddenly and inexplicably sped up as if something had briefly shoved—or dragged—it. Other probes have been affected in the same way.

7. OMG PARTICLE

In 1991 the "Fly's Eye" telescope detected a particle 40 million times more powerful than any other. A few more have been seen since, but nobody knows where all that power comes from.

6. GREEN STARS

If you heat a piece of metal, it will glow red, then orange, then yellow, but never green. The same is true of stars. Yet the star Zubeneschamali (Beta Librae) was once green, according to several astronomers who observed it a century ago.

5. IBEX RIBBON

The *Interstellar Boundary Explorer* satellite studies the very edge of the solar system—and it has found a vast, invisible, ribbon-shaped structure there (right). Particles headed its way bounce back—but what is it?

IBEX-Lo

4. WHY SPIRALS?

Spiral galaxies should behave like the solar system, with the outermost parts rotating slower than those near the middle. But in that case, their spiral arms would soon disappear. But they don't.

1. THE BIG BANG

Nobody knows what caused the Big Bang. This is the greatest mystery of all.

3. MISSING ANTIMATTER

You are made of matter; if you came into contact with antimatter, both you and it would be destroyed. When the universe formed, there should have been equal amounts of both—yet there seems to be no antimatter left. Why not?

2. DARK UNIVERSE

The stars we can see make up only a tiny part of the universe. No one is sure what the rest is made of. The gravity of the stars in other galaxies is too weak to hold the galaxies together, so we can only guess that more gravity comes from dark matter.

TOP TEN
NASA PHOTOS

Since it was formed in 1958, NASA has kept the USA at the forefront of space research. It has sent people to the Moon and to space stations, and probes to planets, comets, asteroids, and moons throughout the solar system. Meanwhile, it has made some of the most famous and beautiful images on Earth.

SATURN

Saturn and its largest moon Titan, and Titan's shadow.

HUBBLE GALLERY

The Hubble Space Telescope (HST) has produced more amazing images than all of the world's other telescopes combined.

CORE OF OMEGA CENTAURI
A star cluster.

ABELL 520
A cluster of distant galaxies.

EXPLODING STAR
Supernova 1987A.

205

APOLLO 11 "EAGLE"

The Apollo 11 "Eagle" lunar module returning from the Moon's surface in 1969.

CHALLENGER SPACE SHUTTLE

The tragic destruction of the *Challenger* Space Shuttle in 1986. Everyone onboard was killed.

BRUCE McCANDLESS

Bruce McCandless making the first ever untethered spacewalk in 1984.

EARTHRISE OVER THE MOON

The Earth rising over the Moon, taken from Apollo 8 in 1968.

ED WHITE

Ed White spacewalking in 1965.

Buzz Aldrin on the Moon

Buzz Aldrin on the Moon in 1969, with Neil Armstrong and the Lunar Module reflected in his visor.

Apollo 15

Lunar module with James Irwin, 1971.

Astronauts

Astronauts working on the ISS in 2010.

Earth

NASA image of the Earth from space, 2002.

Columbia space shuttle

Launch of the first space shuttle, *Columbia*, in 1981.

Author

Dr. Mike Goldsmith is both a working scientist and a writer of science books—mainly for children. His main areas of research are astronomy and sound.

Since 1999, Mike has written over 40 science books. Two were shortlisted for the Royal Society Prize for Science Writing. His books have been published in over 20 countries and cover many areas of science and technology. They have been written for readers of many ages, from toddlers to adults.

Since 1986, Mike has written over 50 papers, reports, and articles about sound, astronomy, and many other science topics. He has been interviewed about noise pollution on Canadian, US, Australian, and UK radio and has given several presentations on the subject and on others, including Einstein and Dark Energy.

Mike lives in Twickenham, near London, England.

Picture Credits